PRECISION SHOOTING HANDBOOK: RIFLE AND HANDGUN

Fundamentals of Marksmanship

Aram Hovasapyan

Aram Hovasapyan

ISBN 13: 979-8-9851063-0-5

Cover design by: Aram Hovasapyan
Printed in the United States of America

Thank you to my parents for supporting me in my hobby while growing up. And thank you to my sister for helping me edit this book.

CONTENTS

PREFACE TO THE SECOND EDITION

I wrote the first edition of this handbook as a side project during the height of the Covid-19 pandemic and nationwide lockdown. From years of shooting and reading and analyzing, I had the general structure of what I wanted to write about in my head, and the entire project from start to finish took one month. It was a great opportunity to focus and do something that I had long wanted to do.

Since publishing though, I've listened to readers' feedback and questions and had a chance to take a look with a fresh eye at how I could improve this book. In this second edition I added new pictures and diagrams to reinforce concepts and expanded the discussion to touch upon some topics that I had not mentioned in the first edition for the sake of brevity. Quite a number of readers also asked me for my recommendations on guns to purchase. In response, I have added a chapter at the end of the book discussing things to consider when shopping for a rifle or handgun as well as a guide on how to mount a scope and sight it in. This handbook now provides the reader a true one-stop, comprehensive reference on shooting fundamentals as well as direction on selecting and setting up their gun for hunting and recreational target shooting.

I also had a chance to check off an item from my bucket list and took a week-long rifle course at the renowned Gunsite Academy in Arizona. It was a great experience where the focus was on field shooting rather than the more traditional match shooting I was used to. The drills and simulators allowed me to rethink certain aspects of my own shooting, and I included some additional tips that I learned from that experience too. And I am proud to say that

I completed the class with a Marksman First Class designation and received the coveted "Silver Raven" pin awarded to the winner of the final shoot-off among class participants, many of whom with military and law enforcement backgrounds.

Finally, I have created Instagram and email accounts at "precisionshootingschool" and "precisionshootingschool@gmail.com," respectively. Please follow and reach out with any questions.

And with that, thanks for reading!

INTRODUCTION

First off, thank you for purchasing this book and for your interest in a wonderful sport. That you intend to read this book means that you appreciate proper marksmanship as a skill necessary to getting the most out of your gun, whether at the shooting range or in the field.

My motivation to write this book is to provide beginner shooters with a concise, but complete, all-in-one resource discussing the fundamentals of shooting both rifles and handguns, as the core concepts for the two are the same.

There seems to be a renewed nationwide interest in firearms and shooting, and people spend a lot of money for the latest guns and gear. But as often happens with other purchases, these new gunowners tend to dedicate much less time and money to learning how to effectively use the instruments they purchased to their full potential. This book attempts to serve as a comprehensive course on shooting fundamentals, suitable for both beginners and more experienced shooters alike.

The concepts and techniques I will cover are neither new nor revolutionary; on the contrary, they are used by every top-level marksman. There are a good number of books and articles on shooting that I have read and recommend and that I refer to in this handbook. Most books, however, are written for either complete beginners and focus on safe gun handling rather than marksmanship fundamentals or they provide incredible detail and analysis more appropriate for an experienced shooter. And of these, handgun and rifle shooting are treated as two separate subjects and rarely appear together in the same book.

In writing this book, I strived for a Goldilocks balance attempting to not leave the porridge too cold with an incomplete overview, but I also tried to not make the porridge too hot by going into possibly overwhelming details. Most importantly, I wanted to explain the *"why"* behind the techniques and methods used with modern, easy to understand examples. I also discuss the benefits of training with airguns and the perfect role they can play in developing and cementing our shooting technique.

Shooting, first and foremost, is an intellectual sport. What Yogi Berra said about baseball applies to shooting as well; it "is 90 percent mental. The other half is physical." To shoot well, we need a basic understanding of human anatomy, a bit of physics, and of how our body interacts with the gun during the shooting process. In a nutshell, that understanding is the secret to good marksmanship.

Throughout this book, I try to demonstrate and drive home the core concepts with everyday examples, such as how the process of taking a picture on your iPhone is directly applicable to good shooting. I also explain multiple ways you can immediately self-diagnose your mistakes, even in the comfort of your living room.

I have used many of these examples and explanations when helping friends and family to develop their shooting, and most often their reaction is, "Ah, that makes sense." I hope that after reading this book, you will walk away with a strong and clear grasp of the concepts and techniques necessary for good shooting. I also hope that this book will serve as just the start of your journey on mastering a captivating, though often challenging, sport. And don't forget, to reach that sometimes elusive level of mastery, like anything else in life, we need to practice, practice, practice.

I want to address one other point right off the bat. This book will not discuss gun safety and safe gun handling practices. I firmly believe that it is the responsibility of every gun owner to learn how to safely operate his/her firearm before even taking one shot out of that gun. For that purpose, the gunowner should refer to the owner's manual and the plethora of good videos on Youtube that address these topics for almost every imaginable firearm.

Finally, a little bit about me, your author. I am not a professional shooter, or ex-military sniper, or anything like that. In fact, my education is in finance and I work in that field. But I became fascinated with the shooting sports almost 15 years ago and have been an ardent student of the sport ever since. I convinced my parents to buy me my first air rifle in middle school (a $100 break-barrel from Big 5), and I became hooked on trying to wring every last drop of precision out of it. As a history buff, I also appreciate the development and impact of firearms throughout history, and fittingly, my first firearm was a World War II era Mosin-Nagant rifle (also at the time $100 at Big 5.) With that rifle - and some motivation from the WW II sniper movie *Enemy at the Gates* - I began exploring the world of long-range shooting. Over the years and over many firearm and airgun purchases, I tried to study every aspect of shooting. For me, it is a favorite hobby to enjoy outside of my day job. It fascinates me how a projectile weighing only a few grams can be directed so precisely and repeatedly to a target hundreds of yards away. I read heavily on the subject, even scavenging online for books no longer in print, and I have competed in local matches when time allowed. The shooting community has always been a welcoming and great resource as well.

To wrap up, shooting is a hobby that I have enjoyed throughout my life. With this book, I hope to pass along what I have learned and my love for the sport to you, the reader. Enjoy, and good shooting!

CHAPTER 1 - AIMING AND SIGHT PICTURE

Pick up an entry level rifle or a handgun and it will usually be equipped with iron sights that consist of a rear sight with a "U" shaped or square shaped notch cut into the center and a front "post" sight. These sights allow us to point our firearm consistently and repeatedly at the target and send a bullet to the mark. Our objective is to "line up" and center the front post inside the notch of the rear sight and to extend that line to the target (see the following diagram). We will refer to this view of how the sights and target appear while aiming the firearm as our "sight picture."

In focus "crystal clear" front sight

Out of focus "blurry" target and bullseye

Out of focus "blurry" rear sight

Center Hold

"6 O'clock" Hold

◆ ◆ ◆

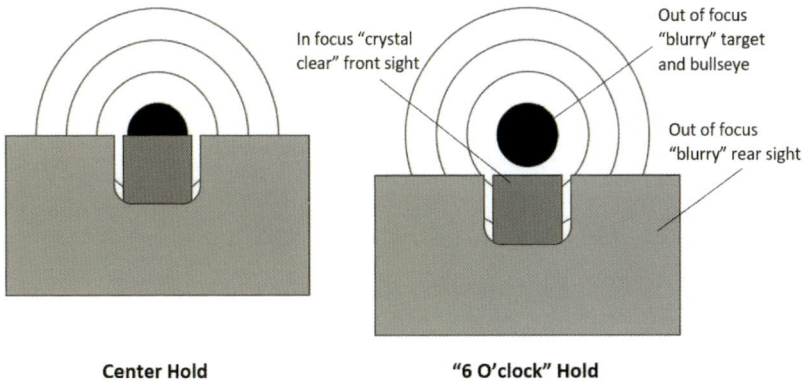

Center Or "6 O'clock" Hold?

There are generally two ways to line up your sights with the target, if the sights on your gun are adjustable. With the center hold (left image), our line of sight cuts the bullseye in half, and the bullet will hit the target right where the tip of our front sight appears on the target – in other words, "dead on" (provided our sights are calibrated accordingly). Alternatively, we can use a "6 o'clock" hold (right image) which essentially lines up the sights as if we were aiming at the six o' clock marker on a clock, but had the sights calibrated such that the bullet would hit the center of the clock (a little bit higher than the tip of the front sight). The center hold is perhaps more instinctive to acquire, but it blocks off half of the bullseye and can make it hard to determine whether we are bisecting the bullseye from the exact center. In the field too, the center hold will invariably obstruct part of the aiming point on our target. The "6 o'clock" hold is the preferred choice for precision shooting, because it is easier for our eye to balance the fully visible bullseye right on top of the front sight than to cut the bullseye exactly in half when part of it is blocked by the front sight. If our sights are correctly calibrated for the 6 o'clock hold, the bullet will strike a little high and into the center of the bullseye. But what if my targets and bullseyes are not all the same size and shape, you ask? Read the "Aim Small, Miss Small" section later in this chapter.

◆ ◆ ◆

Try lining up the sights and aiming at a target in practice, and you'll quickly notice that, try as you might, you aren't able to get the front and rear sights and the target to appear in focus all together. Faced with this dilemma, the beginner shooter will usually focus his/her attention – and eyes – on the target, but then s/he will notice that the sights do not appear sharp and clear. Focus your eyes on the front or the rear sight, and the target and the sight not focused on will appear blurry. What to make of this and why does this happen?

It is because the human eye is very much like the camera lens in your smart phone – it can only focus on one distance at a time (your focal point). Imagine taking a picture of your friend at a concert and wanting to capture your favorite musician on stage in the shot as well. If you tap your friend's face on the phone screen, the stage and musician will appear blurry. And if you tap on the area of the screen where the musician is standing, the camera will focus on the musician, and your friend's face will appear somewhat blurry and pixelated.

Now if we take this analogy back to our aiming exercise, we can understand why our eye cannot focus on all three points at once. The question is, at which of the three points should our eye focus on: the target, the front sight, or the rear sight? **We need to focus with all effort and energy on the front sight so that it appears crystal clear in our sight picture.** Why? Because the front sight is the point furthest out towards the target where we can control the direction the firearm is pointing and the direction the bullet will shoot out. And given that the firearm is always moving in our hands – however marginally – the front sight allows us to register these constant movements relative to the target and to release the shot at the optimal moment. To accomplish this task, the front sight must remain crystal clear. I cannot stress enough how necessary it is for precise shooting to focus on the front sight and keep it sharp and in focus in your sight picture.

As for the target appearing blurry, our eyes can still make out the general contours of a blurry shape and its center just as easily as the contours and the center of a clear one. Pointing at the center of a blurry circle or just below it is essentially no different than pointing at or right below a circle with a clear outline. The same argument can be made about the rear sight. We can precisely position the clearly defined front sight into the center of the notch cut into the rear sight *even* when the notch appears blurry. If your rifle is equipped with an aperture rear sight – as many military type rifles are – then positioning the front post inside the center of the blurry circular aperture is also no problem at all.

To drive the point home, I will point out that perfect vision is not necessary to shoot well, and quite a few Olympic level shooters are near-sighted. Prescription glasses – and shooting glasses (a separate topic outside the scope of this book) - can certainly help, but fundamentally a shooter only needs to be able to see the front sight clearly to shoot precisely.

◆ ◆ ◆

"Aim Small, Miss Small"

In the Revolutionary War epic film *The Patriot*, Mel Gibson's character instructs his sons before a skirmish with British troops to, "aim small, miss small." Excellent shooting advice indeed, despite coming from a movie (perhaps life advice too, but I'll let you be the judge of that). We want to aim at something small and specific – ideally something that appears the same size as our front sight on the target (for example, the brass buttons on British revolutionary era uniforms would have served the purpose for the characters in the movie). By aiming at a precise point on the target, if we miss the point, we will likely still hit the larger target. And let's not forget that shooting is a precision sport. If you are reading this book to be able to shoot more precisely, then you will also understand that in order to do that, you need a precise target.

◆ ◆ ◆

What About Scopes?

Many hunting rifles manufactured nowadays are intended to be used only with telescopic sights (scopes) and do not have any iron sights. The biggest advantage of scopes (besides magnifying our target) is that they allow us to put the image of the target in the same focal plane as the reticle (the crosshairs), so we don't have to worry about which point and distance to focus on anymore. We will see the target and reticle clearly together. Please refer to Chapter 11 for some tips on selecting a scope for your rifle and a guide on how to mount and sight in your scope.

◆ ◆ ◆

CHAPTER 2 - SHOOTING POSITIONS

As you begin to practice proper aiming (be sure to read Chapter 9 for training you can do at home) you will likely be thinking, "I get the importance of focusing on the front sight, Aram, but the front sight is moving around the target non-stop while aiming. I can't get it to settle down." Indeed, there lies the principle challenge and goal of marksmanship - to get the sight picture as steady as possible to fire the perfect shot. And while we will never achieve a completely still sight picture without resting the firearm on an inanimate surface (after all, our living, breathing bodies are never completely still), we can adjust the positioning of our body and our hold of the gun to minimize the movement of the firearm and to steady our sight picture as much as possible.

I have divided this chapter in two sections, beginning with a review of selected positions for shooting rifles followed by the recommended stance for handgun shooting.

RIFLE POSITIONS

Let's begin by recalling how our body reacts when we hold a dumbbell at eye level with our arm fully extended in front of us. If you haven't tried the exercise before, pick up a heavy book or dictionary and hold it out in front of you. After a short while you will feel the tension in your muscles, and as your muscles begin to tire, you will likely notice your arm beginning to tremble. And shortly after that, you will find yourself unable to hold your extended arm at eye level, and your arm will start inching down.

Now with the same dumbbell or book in hand and your arm bent, place your elbow on your hip or on a table with the dumbbell/book pointing up. The weight feels much lighter, and we can maintain this position much longer with our arm remaining steady.

We will take this same concept from the exercise above and apply it to holding a rifle. The average rifle can weigh anywhere from 7 to 10 pounds, and more if equipped with a scope. Aim the rifle while supporting it with just your muscles ("offhand"), and after a few seconds, you will likely find the front sight or the crosshairs wobbling all over the target. And shots taken "offhand" tend to hit low on the target, because just as with the dumbbell, our fatigued supporting arm starts inching down under the weight of the rifle. But aim the rifle with your elbow or arm resting on a bench or on your hip or another bone, and you will achieve a much tighter sight picture without your muscles getting tired.

Therefore, we will assume positions where our skeleton – and not our muscles - will support the weight of the rifle, and hence provide us a much more stable shooting platform and minimum wobble in the sight picture.

Below we will review several widely utilized shooting positions that do not require any external devices or objects to rest the rifle on and can be adapted in various circumstances. These positions take advantage of bone-to-ground or bone-to-bone contact to create a stable platform that will support the weight of the rifle without relying on our muscles. Of course, the aspiring marksman should practice and become competent shooting offhand as well. But as a rule of thumb, we should assume a position that utilizes skeletal support whenever possible and practical due to the inherently steadier sight picture that such a position provides.

In reading through the descriptions and pictures below, focus on understanding *why* a certain position or arm placement aids in our shooting, rather than focusing on exactly replicating the stance I have assumed. Our bodies are all built differently, and we have varying levels of flexibility (I know mine could use some improvement). But if you understand the *why*, you can tailor these positions to your liking and comfort all while taking advantage of the concepts that work to steady your aim. And for more in-depth reading on rifle shooting positions and rifle shooting techniques in general, I highly recommend, *Ways of the Rifle* by Gaby Buhlmann et al and Jeff Cooper's *The Art of the Rifle.*

Finally, you will also notice that in most of the pictures below there is a sling attached to the rifle that loops around my supporting arm. In addition to serving as a convenient means to carry the rifle, a shooting sling is an invaluable aid to shooting precisely. Please refer to the discussion on shooting slings at the end of this section.

Prone:

The prone position is the steadiest position of all since our body and both elbows rest on the ground. Our supporting elbow rests directly - or almost directly - under the rifle to support its weight (this applies to all shooting positions). The orientation of our body to the target is at an angle – around 20-30 degrees is a good compromise between recoil absorption, elbow position, and comfort. To get on target, we can swing around the axis of our hips and can shift the position of our shooting elbow for elevation adjustments. The shortcoming of the prone position is that it isn't useful in very many cases. Because we are so close to the ground, tall grass and brush during a hunt, for example, will obstruct our view of the target.

Sitting:

The sitting position places the shooter and the muzzle of the rifle at a higher line than the prone position, while remaining almost as stable as the prone. I will cover two variations of this position.

Cross-Legged:

This is the classic sitting position shot in some matches and often taught in military marksmanship training. It is the most stable sitting position, because our crossed legs further solidify our foundation and both arms rest on that steady platform. Our body is turned at an angle to the target such that the supporting arm's elbow is positioned right under the rifle when the gun is naturally pointed on target (usually about 45 degrees). An important point to mention is that we do not rest our elbows on our knees (two sharp, unstable points); instead we rest our supporting arm above the elbow across our shin (the larger surface of two flat areas aids in stability), and our shooting arm rests on the inside of the knee. To achieve this placement, we need to lean forward in the sitting position. The issue with the cross-legged variation is that the marksman cannot readily make elevation adjustments and is limited to using the position on flat ground at a target that is around eye level.

Open-Legged:

The open-legged variation is very versatile, since it allows the marksman to shoot at targets at various angles and elevations (just move around your butt to adjust direction and move your feet in and out to adjust for elevation), while providing support for both arms. Notice that, here too, we try to avoid resting the supporting elbow on the knee - my supporting arm is resting just next to the kneecap on the flat surface created by the thigh and shin bones around the knee. The stability and versatility of this position makes it my favorite.

Kneeling:

Along with prone and standing, the kneeling position is one of the three Olympic shooting positions. And it is almost universally the least favored position by competitors because of the pain and discomfort it causes in the rear leg. On top of that, the shooting elbow is left hanging in the air with nothing to rest on, making this position the least stable from the supported positions. It is faster to get into than sitting or prone, but as we'll see, the military squat is even faster. The discomfort plus the lesser stability of this position makes it one that should not be used often in the field.

Military Squat:

I first came across this position in Jeff Cooper's *The Art of the Rifle,* and I really liked its merits. It is a great compromise between speed and stability. As with the other positions, our body's angle to the target is determined by our supporting arm's elbow being directly – or almost directly – under the rifle when we point the gun on target. The supporting arm rests on the front knee (the bent knee exposes a nice, flat area to rest the arm on), while the shooting arm rests on the inside of the rear knee (again, contact is made with the flat surface of the upper arms resting on or inside the knees). We can get into position almost as fast as the time it would take to fire the shot offhand; even while hiking or running, we can just squat down and fire off our shot.

"Olympic" Standing:

This is the position that 10 meter air rifle matches are shot from. The position is more stable than the off-hand position, but is rather awkward and more time consuming to assume. We stand with our feet in line, but directly perpendicular to the target. The key here is that our supporting elbow rests on our hip to provide bone-to-bone contact for support. The fore-ends of match air rifle and smallbore rifle stocks extend down to the level of the trigger guard, making it possible to rest the rifle in our palm or fist and still reach our hip with the supporting elbow. With traditional hunting rifles, this is more difficult, and that is why you see me supporting the rifle from under the trigger guard and stock with my fingers in an extended "V" shape, so that my elbow can reach my hip. Outside of competition, this position is only useful for instances when, due to obstacles in our line of sight, we must remain standing with nothing around to lean against and have the time to assume this position.

Offhand Standing:

The offhand is the least stable of all positions, but without a doubt, it is the fastest. This is the position to shoot from when we must fire off a shot at a moment's notice. In the offhand, we stand at about a 45 degree angle to the target with our supporting arm directly under the rifle, but held up by our muscles. We shoulder the rifle bringing it up to the target, and in a few seconds the shot should go, "BANG." If we have a few seconds more, the military squat is a far more stable position to shoot from.

◆ ◆ ◆

Stocks, Shoulder Pockets, & Cheek Welds

How the stock is positioned and where it contacts our body is a crucial variable for shooting a rifle accurately. The overarching theme that I want to emphasize (and that I will stress again in Chapter 7) is the importance of consistency in our shooting. And to achieve that desired consistency, we need to ensure that we position the gun and aim the same way every time. We want to place the butt of the stock securely against our shoulder pocket (the "pocket" area formed between our shoulder and chest and below our collarbone when we raise our shooting elbow). This stock position will help us effectively absorb the rifle's recoil.

Next, let's place our cheek on the stock's comb. Our cheek's position on the stock will serve as an anchor point and allow us to maintain a consistent line of sight and sight picture shot after shot. This cheek position is referred to as a "cheek weld", the term itself emphasizing the consistent, "welded" placement on the stock. A key point (and one that I try to demonstrate in the previous pictures of shooting positions) is that we should not unnaturally lower our head or cant it sideways to reach the stock; instead, we should adjust the placement of the stock against the body to allow for a comfortable and consistent cheek weld. Notice that in the standing positions, the top part of the buttstock is protruding well above my shoulder, and only the bottom half is making contact with my body. This allows me to achieve a comfortable cheek weld while keeping my head naturally straight. In the sitting or prone positions when my body and head are naturally leaning forward, the stock is placed lower into the shoulder pocket to achieve a comfortable cheek weld. And likewise, achieving a perfectly consistent cheek weld across all shooting positions is unlikely (without an adjustable stock) because of the change in our body geometry from one position to another. Similar to the example above, our body's and neck's natural forward cant in the sitting and prone positions is likely to position our cheek slightly more forward on the stock compared to our cheek weld when standing. But strive to achieve perfect consistency within each shooting position and as much consistency as possible from one position to another.

Additionally, consider purchasing a cheek riser to install on your rifle's stock. This can aid immensely in getting a good cheek weld when shooting a scoped rifle. And some rifles (like the synthetic stocked Weatherby I'm aiming with in some of the previous pictures) already have a "built-in" cheek riser in the form of a "Monte Carlo" comb, a raised design intended specifically for use with scopes.

◆ ◆ ◆

Gunslinger - The Shooting Sling

Use of the shooting sling can dramatically stabilize our shot when shooting from a supported position (supporting arm resting on our body, the ground, or another hard surface). Jeff Cooper, a strong proponent for using a sling, explained its function beautifully. "The function of the shooting sling is to take the weight off the muscles of your support arm, so that when you are in a proper firing position you can relax all your muscles and the weapon will remain exactly on target." By running from the fore-end of the stock across our forearm and looping around the upper arm, the sling essentially "ties" the two branches of the "V" that our supporting arm creates to each other and to the rifle so that we no longer need to rely on muscle support to hold the rifle. The benefit is huge; the muscles that could disturb our shot can now be "turned off" and the rifle will still point exactly on target. The sling that I have attached on my rifle is a "Rhodesian Sling" available from Andy's Leather. I find it much faster to sling up compared to a traditional military style sling and yet almost as stable.

Let's also briefly discuss sling position on the upper arm, because once you try to sling up a few times the question will invariably cross your mind. The traditional approach tells us to loop the sling as high and tight on the upper arm as possible. While this makes sense as the most secure location to "tie" the "V", in my experience it also puts the most pressure on the artery in the upper arm and can lead to our pulse beats being transferred as movement in the rifle. Hence, I prefer a midway point on the upper arm as a compromise.

Another point to note is that if we intend to sling up in the field and fire a shot from various positions at a moment's notice, then the sling should be pre-set at an intermediate length, and we can fine tune for appropriate tension by adjusting the position of the loop on the upper arm. For example, shooting from prone where the supporting arm and body is extended further and the "V" stretched open will likely require us to lower the sling on the arm, while we can raise it higher on the arm when shooting from a more contracted position like sitting or kneeling to maintain the appropriate tension and support for the rifle. It may also help to mark the holes on our sling for adjustments based on the thickness of clothing we are wearing, such as for heavy winter gear.

Finally, you'll notice in the pictures that I am not using the sling while aiming offhand. This is because in the offhand position our arms are not resting on any stable surface, and we must rely on our muscles to support the weight of the rifle. Any added tension from a sling will not help us here. Instead, I scoop the sling up under the rifle in my support hand to avoid the loose sling potentially swinging side to side and thus swaying the rifle and distorting my aim.

◆ ◆ ◆

HANDGUN POSITIONS

For shooting a handgun, I will limit our discussion to assuming a stance that utilizes a two-handed hold of the firearm, since the advantages of a two-handed vs single-handed hold for practical shooting are now widely accepted. However, athletes in Olympic pistol shooting disciplines are restricted to holding their handgun with one hand only, and the level of precision they display is remarkable. If you would like to learn more about Olympic style pistol shooting, the book *Pistol Shooting, The Olympic Disciplines* by Heinz Reinkemeier and Gaby Buhlmann is an excellent and incredibly detailed resource on the subject.

To assume a two-handed shooting position, stand facing straight towards the target in a relaxed, natural stance with your feet shoulder width apart, knees just slightly bent, and your shoulders rolled slightly forward, making it easier to absorb recoil. We want a stable and relaxed platform, free from muscle tension. Now the key idea to understand in a two-handed stance is the role and purpose of the support hand. **It is there to support the weight of the handgun.** This should come as no surprise. We discussed that when shooting a rifle, the purpose of our non-shooting arm is to serve as a platform to rest the rifle on and to support its weight, and this is exactly the case with the handgun as well. As Albert League writes in *The Perfect Pistol Shot*, an excellent book, "The primary function of the support hand is to provide a load-bearing platform that enables the shooting hand to shift from weightlifting to sight alignment adjustments and trigger press." To reiterate, whether shooting a rifle or handgun, the concept is the same.

Finally, let's grip the handgun with our shooting hand (we will discuss the elements of a proper shooting hand grip in detail in the next chapter) and use our supporting arm to lift the handgun and our shooting hand up to eye level and pointing at the target. My preferred method of doing this - which I discovered through trial and error - is to lightly wrap my supporting hand around my shooting hand and push up on the trigger guard with the top of my supporting hand's index finger, thus bearing the weight of the handgun and lifting it up from around its center of gravity. Another alternative is to "scoop" up the butt of the handgun and shooting hand with the supporting hand and lift them up together. Either way, the objective is to create a weight-bearing platform for the handgun to rest on. Otherwise, a two-handed hold would provide no advantage over a single-handed hold.

A final point I would like to address: I stressed that we want to avoid taking shots with a rifle offhand and instead assume positions stabilized by our skeletons. And yet with the handgun position above, the supporting arm, and thus the handgun, is held up by our muscles. While I encourage the shooter to rest his/her arms on a solid surface when possible, in most cases, a handgun is fired from the standing position with nothing to rest on nearby and no time to assume a supported position (prone, Creedmoor, etc). That the handgun has historically been referred to as a sidearm points to the fact that it often served as a back-up and a weapon of last resort. And in such a scenario, the two-handed stance I described is the most stable position to assume.

CHAPTER 3 - GRIP AND TRIGGER PRESS

GRIP

It should come as no surprise to the reader from reading the prior chapter that I will advocate for as relaxed a grip on the gun as possible. Why? Again, because we want to limit the tension in our muscles from adversely affecting our shooting. The less we humans "interfere" with the gun and apply uneven pressure, the better.

I will start with discussing the proper grip for handguns and then rifles.

Let's briefly revisit the example from the first chapter where we were trying to take a picture of our friend at a concert. When taking a picture, we hold our iPhone with a relaxed grip - just strong enough not to drop the phone. If we held the phone with a crushing grip around it, our hand would tremble, and the picture would come out blurry. If we translate this back to shooting, a tight and tense grip of the gun would result in additional movement in our sight picture and a less precise shot.

To be clear, I am not advocating for a limp grip, the grip we will assume will be deliberate, but free from any unnecessary tension.

To assume the proper grip, we start by gripping the handgun with our shooting hand as high on the handgun's backstrap as possible (see the following picture). Next, with our middle finger, we press the handgun straight back into the web of our hand, trying to place the barrel as much in line with our forearm as possible; the barrel and forearm will not align completely in a forward-facing stance, but the closer you can get it, the better. This barrel to forearm alignment coupled with the high grip will make it easier for us to absorb the gun's recoil.

At this point, the only pressure on the handgun should be coming from the middle finger pressing straight back, and the gun should be fully secured between the middle finger and the web of our hand. Any other pressure from our remaining fingers has the potential to create uneven and sideways tension, resulting in a "pulled" shot. With our ring finger and pinky, we can press the grip directly rearward into the web of our hand as we did with our middle finger, being mindful not to apply any sideways pressure. Or we can gently wrap those last two fingers around the grip and let them just come "along for the ride," as I recall Tom Gaylord, known as the "Godfather of Airguns," phrasing it once in his video blog that I was watching when picking up the sport. The thumb, which always exerts sideways pressure when we grip any object, should naturally point forward parallel to the barrel and only lightly touch the grip without applying any pressure on the gun (you can lift the thumb completely off the gun as well).

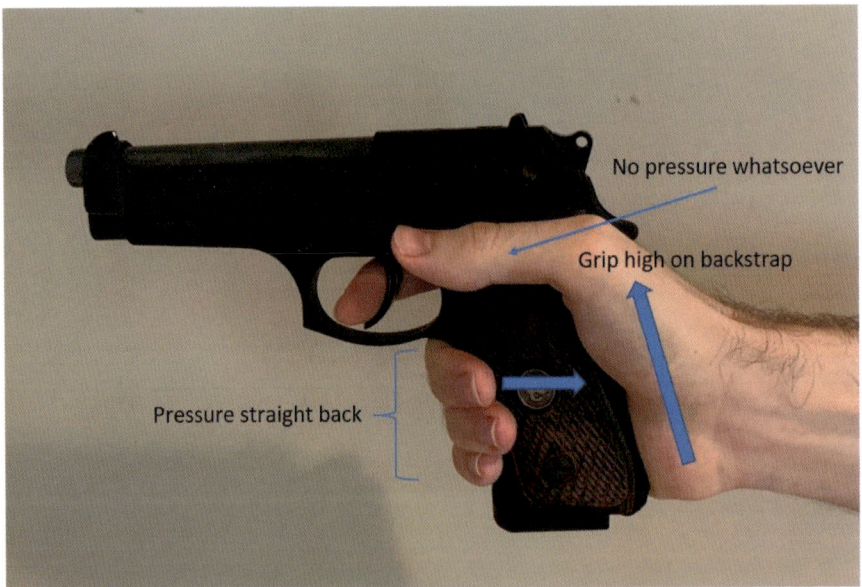

And now that the handgun is secured in our shooting hand, our trigger finger is free to perform its sole - and crucial – function: a clean, smooth trigger press.

The same concept applies regarding the proper grip for a rifle. When shooting without a sling, the middle, ring, and pinky fingers of our shooting hand press the rifle directly rearward into our shoulder pocket. The weight of the rifle is supported by our non-shooting arm, and the butt of the rifle is positioned securely against our body to absorb the recoil. You'll notice in the preceding pictures that the thumb of the shooting hand lies on top of the stock without applying any pressure, because just like while gripping a pistol, we don't want the thumb exerting any sideways pressure.

If a sling is used, there is no need for the shooting hand to apply any rearward pressure; the rifle should securely stay in place even if the shooting hand is completely taken off the rifle. Therefore, a strong grip around the stock by the shooting hand provides no benefit and will only add to the risk of pulling the shot through uneven pressure.

◆ ◆ ◆

Holding On For Dear Life

Over-gripping is a common error by beginner shooters who are concerned that recoil is going to send the handgun flying out of their hands. Don't worry! With a proper grip – even a light one – that won't happen. Brian Enos drives the point home in his excellent and comprehensive book, *Practical Shooting, Beyond Fundamentals*. He stresses, "Muscle tension does not provide recoil control...Recoil recovery is only possible through exercising the fundamentals of position, timing, and relaxation." A good rule of thumb (no pun intended) is that if any of your fingernails turn white, then you are over-gripping.

Also, over-gripping tends to throw our shots inside and low. So, a right-handed shooter's shots would likely hit low and left of the target center and a left-handed shooter's shots would hit low and right. Before you start tinkering with the sights, consider that the problem might not be with the gun, but with the shooter behind the gun.

◆ ◆ ◆

The "Artillery Hold"

Spring piston air rifles (among them the "break-barrels" you've likely seen at sporting goods stores) are known to have a quite bizarre recoil pattern (they first recoil forward as the spring uncoils and then backwards as the pellet is leaving the muzzle-and vibrate throughout the process). Because airgunners want to make sure that throughout the double recoil and vibration the muzzle moves and points exactly the same way from shot to shot, they hold the rifle very gently and let it almost "float" in their hands. This way the rifle settles into its own repeatable cycle, with minimal human interference. Tom Gaylord gave it the name "artillery hold" because the hold tries to replicate the way barrels of artillery pieces freely move back within the gun carriage during recoil. Luckily, most firearms are less sensitive to how they are held compared to airguns. And I don't recommend you practice the artillery hold with a magnum centerfire rifle, because you will be left with a rude awakening and likely a bruised shoulder. On the contrary, I think a sling that firmly presses the butt of the rifle against the shoulder pocket is the best way to go. But the core concept carries forward to firearms as well; any unnecessary human influence only increases the risk of a bad shot.

◆ ◆ ◆

TRIGGER PRESS

Now let's scrutinize what a clean trigger press consists of.

Our objective is to press and release the trigger without disturbing our aiming and sight picture. To accomplish that, we need to press the trigger straight to the rear, doing so smoothly and continuously. We want to avoid sideways motion and pressure as much as possible. This is challenging because our fingers pivot in arc like motions – not straight back and forth ones - around our joints. The trigger finger should pivot around the last finger joint, the one closest to the knuckle. Despite the challenge of pressing straight back, the important thing is that the pressure must be directed straight to the rear at the moment when the trigger "breaks." Any pressure to either side at this critical point and the shot will likely stray to the side.

As you may have noticed, your trigger is likely a "two-stage" trigger (as most triggers are) with a light first stage "take up" (where it feels like there is some slack in the trigger) followed by a heavier second stage press that ultimately results in the trigger release. If so, take up the first stage as you are bringing the gun to the target, and you will find yourself entering the tricky world of the second stage trigger press.

Again, we want to apply rearward pressure on the trigger as evenly and continuously as possible until the trigger breaks. You might be tempted to stage the final release at the precise moment when the sights or reticle are exactly aligned with the center of the bullseye (or directly under it, if using a 6 o'clock hold), but this is a futile exercise. It will most often result in a jerk and a pulled shot. The reason staging doesn't work as intended is because the sights are constantly moving around and through the center of the target as we are aiming; these are miniscule movements, yet jagged and sharp when we look at them in slow motion (see the following diagram). By the time our brain sends the signal to our finger to press the trigger at what we perceive to be the ideal time and by the time the finger presses that last bit to the trigger release, the sights will have moved away from that "ideal" center point.

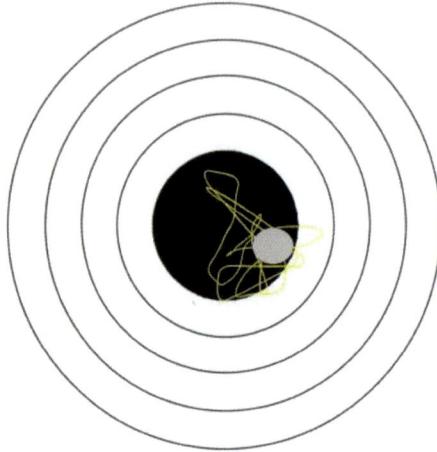

Aiming trace

◆ ◆ ◆

Slo-Mo

The diagram above is a slow-motion view of the aiming trace on the target, assuming a center hold. Even in the final moments before the trigger release, the sights and gun are moving erratically across the target. Our brains, however, only have the capacity to process and react to the general direction and area of these movements. Notice that, in this diagram, the gun was pointing predominantly in the bottom right portion of the bullseye, and the shot ultimately landed in that area.

◆ ◆ ◆

The solution is to practice keeping our hold steady and to keep the movements of the sights around the bullseye in as small an area as possible while applying continuous pressure on the trigger until the shot breaks. As the authors of *Pistol Shooting, The Olympic Disciplines* point out, "From a purely statistical perspective, the ratio of nines to tens....is roughly the same as the ratio of time the gun is pointing at these areas, provided of course that the release doesn't impact on the aiming path."

A lot of folks in shooting circles say to "let it surprise you," when talking about the moment during the trigger press that the trigger is released. Though the intention of the statement is correct, I think it might create some confusion for beginners. After all, if we practice the same motion hundreds or thousands of times, it is hard to be taken completely by surprise again and again. Instead, I once heard the process of the trigger press described as a "consciously unconscious" release, and I think that is the most accurate description of the process. It is conscious in that we knowingly press the trigger evenly and continuously – it doesn't just happen. But at the same time, it is unconscious, since our concentration and focus are on the front sight and on holding as steadily and closely around the center of the bullseye as possible. Again from *Pistol Shooting*, "Trainers talk about firing the shot, *'unconsciously' in the aiming area* – as long as the sights are in the right areas, pressure is increased until the shot is fired."

One final point I want to discuss, since new shooters often ask the question: Which part of the finger should we press the trigger with, the pad or the first joint closest to the tip of the finger? The answer is that you should use the section of the finger that best allows you to apply a smooth trigger press directly to the rear. A couple points to consider though are that the pad of the finger is one of the most sensitive parts of our body and is well-suited to feel and regulate a smooth press. On the other hand, since the first joint is closer to the pivot point of the trigger finger (remember, this is the joint closest to the knuckle) than the pad is, it will feel to us that we need to apply less force to release the trigger.

To better visualize this concept, put your hand in front of you with your palm open and wrist straight, and try holding a full grocery bag first with the straps of the bag around your palm and then with the straps around your fingertips only. It feels harder to keep your wrist (the pivot point in this example) straight when the straps are around your fingertips (further from the pivot) than when they are around your palm (closer to the pivot), even though the weight of the bag did not change. In using the first joint, we are bringing the part of the finger pressing the trigger closer to the pivot point of the finger. I prefer to use the pad of my finger when shooting my hunting rifles and airguns that have light triggers, but I revert to using my first joint when shooting my Beretta pistol – a service grade handgun with a heavier trigger.

In summary, you should now recognize the goal and purpose of a smooth, gradual, and continuous trigger press to the rear and should feel compelled to adjust as necessary to achieve that.

CHAPTER 4 - BREATHING

We have spent a lot of time discussing the adverse effects of muscle movements on our shooting - and we are not done yet! Our breathing, controlled by the diaphragm muscle, is also a major source of movement that we need to work around when shooting.

To visualize the magnitude of movement caused by normal breathing, hold your arms out in front of you as if you were gripping and aiming a handgun, and just breathe. You will notice your hands rise with each inhale and fall with each exhale; the movement will be slight with normal breathing but will be surprisingly noticeable with deeper breaths. I think you will agree that, to prevent these movements, it will be beneficial to our shooting to hold our breath when aiming and through to the trigger release. Let us discuss the best way to do this.

The widely accepted method is to take a breath, let half of it out, and to hold our breath throughout the trigger press and release. There is good reason for holding our breath with our lungs half-full. If you try holding your breath with your lungs completely full of air or after fully exhaling, it will likely feel rather uncomfortable and lead to some shaking in your hold.

And now we must integrate our breathing with the rest of the shooting cycle. In 10 meter air pistol matches, you will see the competitors take a deep breath as they lift their pistols slightly over the target and exhale half of it as they lower their pistols to the target. From there, they hold their breath until the shot is fired.

I think this sequence can serve as a guideline for general

shooting as well. We begin by breathing normally as we get into position, then take a deep breath as we are bringing the gun to target, and then let part of it out as we begin the aiming process and trigger press. From here on until the shot breaks, we must hold our breath (a period that should ideally take around 4 to 8 seconds). If we have not fired the shot after 10 seconds of holding our breath, we should stop, breathe in and out to resupply our body with oxygen, and start the trigger press all over again. Do not keep going with your breath held, as your body and arms will no longer be able to stay as still, and you will likely miss the target.

Of course, such unlimited, leisurely timing may only be afforded to us at the shooting range. But the concept applies in the field too; hold your breath in the few seconds you may have to aim and fire off a shot.

CHAPTER 5 - NATURAL POINT OF AIM

Now that we have covered all the basics of the shooting process and started putting them to practice, we may find ourselves correctly assuming a shooting position, aiming with a crystal clear front sight in our sight picture, pressing off a perfect trigger release, and still hitting to one side or the other of the bullseye and sometimes high or low (this is assuming of course that our sights are zeroed in and in the absence of external factors, like wind). It seems that we are doing everything right, but the bullet just won't consistently hit the center of the target. It almost feels like the rifle or handgun is teasing us. What could be the cause of this phenomenon and how should we address it? The answer lies with examining our "natural point of aim."

To uncover the problem, assume a shooting position with gun in hand, and aim at the target. When your sights are pointed straight at the bullseye, close your eyes and completely relax your body. Keep your eyes closed for about 5 to 10 seconds to ensure that your body is totally relaxed and muscles fully loosened. From reading the previous chapters, we learned that we want to avoid muscle tension as much as possible. But our eyes can subconsciously guide our muscles to "pull" our arms and the firearm towards the target, and this process can be so subtle that we might not even realize that our muscles are at work. With our eyes closed, this guide switches off and our muscles fully relax.

Next open your eyes and note where the sights are now pointing. Most likely, they will be pointing quite a ways from the target. That point where the sights are pointing after your muscles fully relaxed is your body's natural point of aim. Our goal now is to align our natural point of aim with the target. To do that, we need to adjust our body's position and retest where our natural point of aim shifts to by repeating the exercise above.

If you are standing, adjust the position of your feet relative to the target; do not twist your torso, as that will create tension in your muscles. If you are sitting, then you will likely need to adjust the angle at which your body is facing towards the target. And in the prone position, we can shift our body around the axis of our hips and then adjust the position of the shooting arm elbow for more minute corrections. This is an exercise of trial and error and usually requires a coarse adjustment followed by several small incremental ones.

To better visualize why the bullet misses the bullseye in the opening scenario of the chapter, let's think of our body in its relaxed state as an uncoiled spring. If our position is not naturally pointing exactly towards the target, our muscles slightly and subtly "coil" the spring (our body) using muscle tension to get our arms to point the firearm at the target. A shooter unaware of the "natural point of aim" concept will likely not even realize that his muscles are deviously at play.

However, the moment immediately after the shot is fired, this shooter's muscles will likely subconsciously relax thinking that the deed is done and there is no reason to exert any force to keep the gun pointing at the target. As the human spring is "uncoiling", the bullet is still traveling down the barrel for a few fractions of a second after shot is fired. And the direction the body "uncoils" during the bullet's path through the barrel is the direction that the shot will stray.

To avoid the scenario above, we need to practice aligning our natural point of aim with the target from multiple shooting positions. With enough practice, immediately assuming a position almost in line with the target will become second nature. As for the final minor adjustments, that is something even athletes at the highest level at times struggle with. But that level of adjustment and precision is necessary – and practical - only for competition shooting.

CHAPTER 6 - FOLLOW THROUGH

Most athletes in other sports – be it boxing or basketball or something else – as part of their training replay videos of themselves engaging in the sport to self-evaluate and critique their own technique, catch mistakes, and improve their skills. In shooting, the concept of "follow through" serves the same purpose.

Follow through is the process of continuing to maintain our hold and position and our laser focus on the front sight for a second or two *after* the shot has been fired. In doing so, we can evaluate our shot and glean valuable information to then help us improve our shooting. In shooting, unlike most other sports, this self-evaluation happens live as we are firing the shot. This means that we can apply the "feedback" from the follow through process on our very next shot! As we'll see, the marksman that diligently follows through on his shots is rewarded with valuable, actionable information that places him at an incredible advantage over the shooter that is unaware of the concept or doesn't utilize it properly.

However, follow through serves one other purpose that makes the process mandatory for good shooting and not just a "nice to know." Let's start with this point and then talk about the role follow through plays in self-diagnosing our shot.

I briefly mentioned in the last example of Chapter 5 that the bullet stays in the barrel for a short instance after the shot has been fired. What happens is that once the trigger has been released, the firing pin hits the primer on the cartridge, thus causing a mini-explosion inside the chamber that then sends the bullet racing through and out of the barrel. And the opposite reaction is that the gun recoils back toward the shooter but, finding the path "blocked" by our shoulder or the web of our hand, the energy is redirected and sends the muzzle jumping up. Though the whole process takes mere fractions of a second and is over in a blink of an eye, it spans enough time to throw the shot if the shooter is not following through. (The time the bullet spends in the barrel varies depending on the caliber, the ammunition, and the firearm, and we will briefly discuss this topic in Chapter 10.)

If we understand that the bullet remains in the barrel for long enough after the trigger release to affect the result of the shot, then we will also understand that we must continue maintaining our same position, hold, posture, and breath even for a few moments after the trigger has been released so that the shot is not "disrupted" in these final moments. In essence, we are seeing the shot through. Many beginner shooters just let their arms drop immediately after releasing the trigger or immediately peer toward the target in search of the hole the bullet left, but we now know that these are serious errors.

Let's now turn to the second purpose of following through. As I stated, the process of following through provides us with a wealth of information, as long as we don't blink through it. If we stay laser focused on the front sight through the shot firing and the subsequent recoil, we will note the front sight jump up during recoil. If the front sight (or the scope's reticle) jumps up and falls back to rest in the exact position where it was right before the shot broke, then we will know that we fired a "good" shot. Everything was relaxed and in harmony, and there was no uneven tension running through our fingers, arms, or body (no uncoiling of the spring).

But if the front sight jumps up and lands to either side of where it was right before the shot went off, then it could mean that our natural point of aim was not aligned with the target. Or that we were over-gripping or not pressing the trigger straight to the rear, and the gun jerked to the side as the trigger "broke." The important thing is that we know immediately whether our shot was a good one or not, and from what we learned so far in the book, we are aware of the variables that could have contributed to a less than perfect shot. We can then, by process of elimination, calmly check our natural point of aim, our grip, and so on, and take the next shot. We are constantly processing the feedback from the firearm and taking the necessary steps to correct any shortfalls.

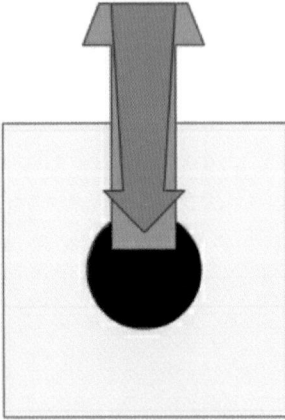

A perfect muzzle jump   The result of some mistake

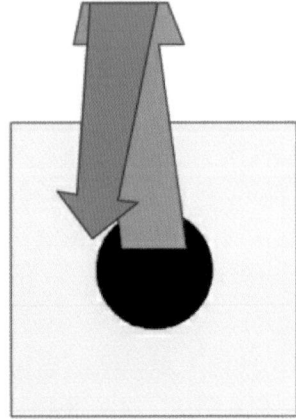

After some practice, we will also be able to accurately call our shots, without having to search for the last hole made in the target. In theory, if we fired a good, clean shot (verified by follow through of course), then where the front sight was pointing right before the trigger release is where the bullet should have hit. If on the other hand, after firing the shot the front sight comes to rest somewhere other than where it was right before the shot went off, then the bullet likely hit someplace between those two points.

One final note: to avoid blinking when the shot goes off and missing this abundance of information offered when properly following through, I recommend wearing good hearing protection when shooting. Our eyes naturally blink upon hearing the loud "BANG" of a firearm, and dampening the noise will also reduce our tendency to blink.

In summary, following through unveils the mystery surrounding the results of our shooting. And to the intelligent marksman this feedback the gun provides is an opportunity to further refine his/her skills.

CHAPTER 7 - RHYTHM AND REPETITION

We have now reviewed all the components of the shooting "puzzle" and even how the pieces connect to one another. All that remains is to put it all together.

Go on YouTube and watch an Olympic shooting match - be that air pistol, air rifle, free pistol, or even the shotgun matches for that matter – and one thing should catch your eye. From shot to shot, the sequence of motion is always the same. The time spent to lift the gun, the moment to inhale and exhale, the time to aim, and the time to release the trigger and send the shot downrange remains fascinatingly unchanged throughout the duration of the match. You can even fast forward a part of the match, and when you resume watching, you likely will not be able to tell that you skipped a portion unless you are following the scores. These top athletes look like they are riding on autopilot. I mention this to demonstrate that **the secret to consistently good shooting is rhythm and repetition.**

This means that to become truly consistent "crack shots," we must train to find a shooting pattern, a sequence of steps, that works for us and produces good results (the general outline of which the previous chapters of this book attempted to provide). And most importantly, once that "working formula," that rhythm is established, we must take special care to perform each step the same way each time. From the way we get into our shooting position and all the way through to the trigger release and follow through, we must strive to repeat each step the same way from shot to shot. And this rhythm should be practiced, established, and maintained for each shooting position; there are no shortcuts.

Of course, we might make incremental changes to our shooting as we practice and improve and notice new details that we hadn't noticed before. That is only natural. But the point of the message remains; consistency and repetition are the secrets to success (in shooting at least, since I am not here to impart life advice.) And I'll add that rhythm is not limited to competition shooters. It has a very realistic application in the field and in self-defense as well, since it will kick our shooting process into autopilot even in high-stress scenarios.

To drive the point home, I will quote Einstein. He said, "Insanity is doing the same thing over and over and expecting different results." I will argue that the converse of that is also true. It is also insane to do something differently each time and expect the same result. **To consistently shoot well, we must shoot consistently.**

CHAPTER 8 - TRAJECTORY

Any discussion on shooting fundamentals would be incomplete without at least briefly discussing the path of the bullet that we are trying to direct with all our diligence towards the center of our target. And to understand trajectory, we need to cover some basic physics (kinematics).

The crucial concept to understand is that bullets travel in parabolic arcs when they leave the muzzle, not in laser-like straight lines. To better visualize this, let us consider an example. Please refer to the Trajectory diagram on the following page as we review the example. The proportions of the diagram are exaggerated for illustrative purposes, but the concept is accurate (the axis markings are quite accurate as well).

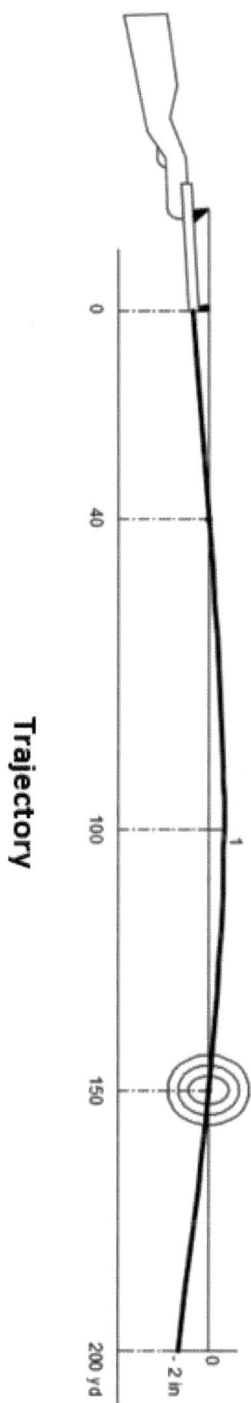

Trajectory

Let's assume that the target we are shooting at is positioned at eye level (not an uncommon scenario) and is 150 yards away. If our sights are properly calibrated for that distance, the barrel of the gun will actually be tilted up above horizontal when we line up our sights with the target. If you are wondering why this is, consider what would happen if the barrel was held exactly horizontally (parallel to flat ground) and at the same height as the target. Because the force of gravity always acts towards the center of the earth (a fancy way of saying straight down), a bullet shot straight horizontally will begin falling from the moment it leaves the muzzle. And 150 yards later, it will either be in the dirt or flying well below our target (this depends on the bullet's velocity). To compensate for the constant force of gravity, we must shoot the bullet up and rely on gravity to pull the bullet down the same way shot after shot (again, provided that we use ammunition with consistent velocity).

In the picture above, I adjusted the rear sight on my Mosin-Nagant rifle to the maximum 2,000 meter range for illustrative purposes (military rifles often have range markings cut into the rear sight allowing for a rough calibration at marked distances, though 2,000 meters is incredibly optimistic and unrealistic). Notice that when the sights are lined up together along the horizontal line of the flooring, the gun is pointing up at a significant angle. In order to cover that extremely long distance while fighting the force of gravity, the bullet must be shot quite a bit upwards. It is no different than throwing a football to your buddy standing across the field. For the football to reach your buddy, you would have to throw it at an upwards angle.

This fact then leads us to another realization. When shooting at distances quite a ways out, the bullet intersects the line of sight twice: once on its way up and once on its way down. If we consider a .308 Winchester caliber rifle sighted in at 150 yards, the bullet will first cross the line of sight around 40 yards from the muzzle, then continue climbing to its highest point about an inch above the line of sight at around 100 yards, then start falling until it re-crosses the line at 150 yards and continue its journey down. This is very useful information for the hunter, because the hunter will know that at any distance out to 200 yards, s/he can aim point blank and will always be within a 2 inch radius from the center of the target (see Trajectory diagram).

Another useful conclusion is that, if our local shooting range is limited to a short distance, we can easily sight in our rifle at 40 yards, knowing that the trajectory will be the same as if it was sighted in at 150 yards (see Trajectory diagram). Also, if the deviations seem small, it is because the .308 Win is a relatively fast, flat shooting round. But at further distances and especially with slower calibers, trajectory plays a crucial part in hitting targets at various distances. Luckily, there are many easy to use online trajectory calculators where we can provide inputs on the rifle, caliber, and desired zero distance, and the tool will plot the bullet's trajectory.

Finally, this trajectory analysis should help us realize the importance of holding our rifle level (vertically straight and not canted) when aiming. When the rifle is held canted our shots will land low and to the side, even if our sights are lined up perfectly with the bullseye. To better visualize why this is, let's turn back to the picture of the Mosin-Nagant on the floor and turn the book sideways as if we were trying to line up the sights with the rifle held sideways (canted at a full 90 degrees to the left). This will help us arrive at two conclusions. First, we can see that the shot will land way off to the left because the previously upward slope of the barrel is now pointed sideways in the direction of the cant.

And second, the shot will land low because, similarly, there is no remaining upward slope in the barrel to counteract the force of gravity. This is an extreme example of course, and the effect of a slight cant at short distances will be negligible but it will cause our point of impact to drift as distance increases.

One other concept I want to briefly discuss relates to shooting uphill and downhill, as this is a scenario which hunters should be familiar with. It is often referred to as the "Rifleman's Rule." Let's assume that a target is again placed 150 yards away from us, except this time on a hill with a 30-degree gradient (refer to the following diagram). Let us also assume, as in the previous example, that the rifle was sighted in at a horizontal distance of 150 yards. Our initial instinct may be that we need to aim a bit higher than the center of the target to compensate for the uphill angle. But instead, we should be doing the exact opposite and aiming below the center of the target!

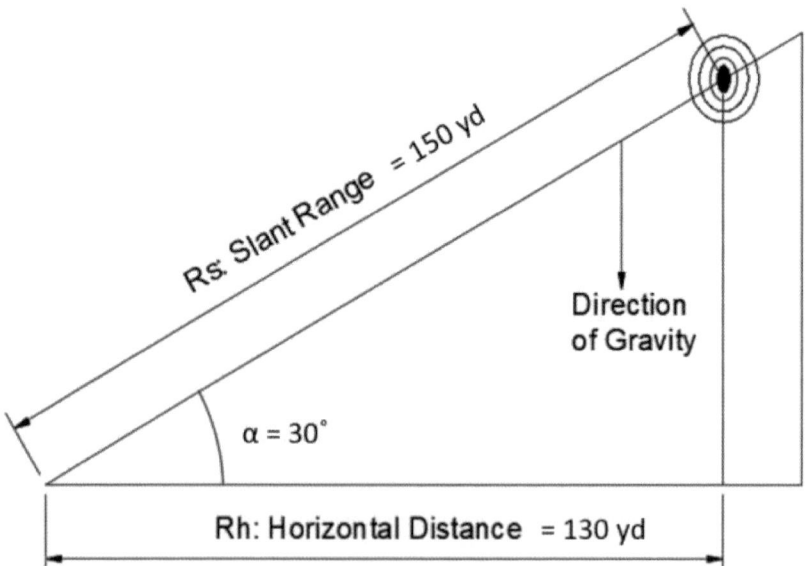

Rs: Slant Range = 150 yd

Direction of Gravity

$\alpha = 30°$

Rh: Horizontal Distance = 130 yd

Rifleman's Rule

Why, you ask? It is once again because of the effects of our friend gravity. Recall that gravity pulls the bullet towards the center of the Earth (straight down). It doesn't care what kind of terrain the bullet traverses or at what angle, instead its impact on the bullet's trajectory depends on the horizontal distance the bullet covers, in other words the distance "as the crow flies." To better visualize this, tie a string around the tip of a pencil and tie a weight at the end of the string. Now hold that pencil from the other tip and at an angle to the floor. If you slide the string up and down the pencil and change the angle you are holding the pencil at, the string remains exactly perpendicular to the flat floor, because gravity is acting straight down. And the steeper the angle you hold the pencil at, the shorter the horizontal distance the weight covers when you slide the string up and down the pencil. Finally, we can experiment and see that the Rifleman's rule applies just the same if the pencil is held at a downward angle (if we are shooting downhill).

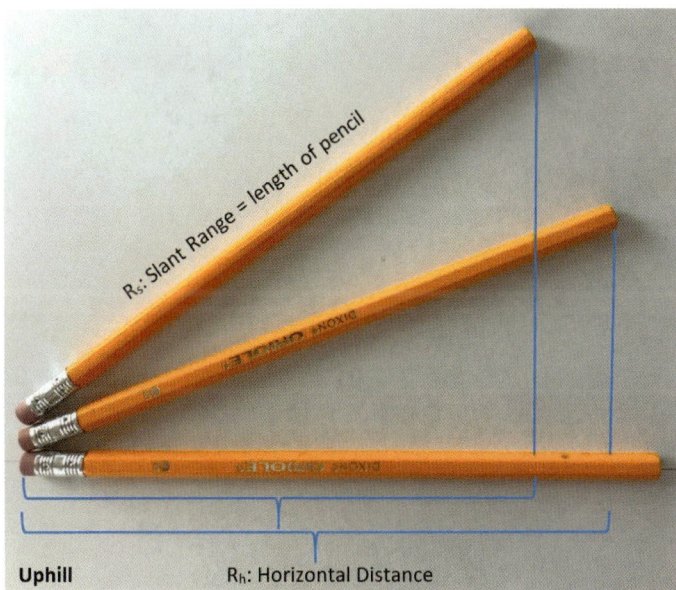

R_s: Slant Range = length of pencil

Uphill R_h: Horizontal Distance

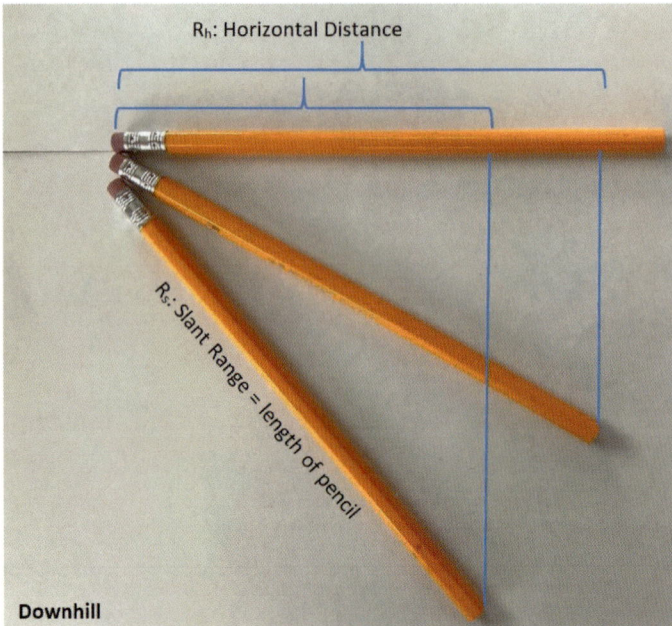

R_h: Horizontal Distance

R_s: Slant Range = length of pencil

Downhill

The two preceding diagrams will also help visualize this concept. All the pencils are of the same length. The steeper the angle of each pencil is relative to horizontal, then the shorter the horizontal distance covered by that pencil. And the horizontal distance covered by a pencil placed at any angle relative to horizontal will always be shorter than the full length of the pencil.

Returning to our example, the 150 yard distance to the target on the hill (R_s) translates to a shorter horizontal distance that the bullet will cover, namely 130 yards. (If you recall from high school trigonometry, the horizontal distance R_H can be calculated as $R_S \cos(\alpha)$.) And if we aimed at the center of the target, the bullet would hit slightly above the center, because at 130 yards, the bullet is still flying above the line of sight (see Trajectory diagram). To exactly hit the bullseye, the marksman must aim low by the same amount that the bullet is above the line of sight at the 130 yard mark of its trajectory (less than an inch in our example). Don't worry, you don't need to remember sines and cosines, the online trajectory calculators I mentioned will do the math for you.

For full disclosure, trajectory and long-range shooting are incredibly detailed subjects, and I have simplified my examples to illustrate the main concepts. In reality, trajectory is determined by many variables beginning from the height of the sights above the bore of the barrel to bullet shape, coefficients of friction, twist rate of the rifling, and even the rotation of the Earth at extreme distances. One can find many books dedicated solely to this subject.

◆ ◆ ◆

"Don't Fire Until You See The Whites Of Their Eyes, And Then Fire Low."

These words are usually credited to General Israel Putnam during the Battle of Bunker Hill when he was giving orders to Continental troops positioned atop a hill and awaiting an attack from British infantry. We can see that in issuing the second part of his order, he had the Rifleman' rule in mind. With the much slower muzzle velocity of Revolutionary era flintlocks – and thus much more pronounced parabolic trajectory – the downhill shots of American troops aiming at the Redcoats' heads risked whizzing completely over them.

◆ ◆ ◆

CHAPTER 9 - DRY FIRING

The best place to practice and hone your shooting is in your living room! Are you surprised by this statement? I stressed the importance of rhythm and repetition in developing good shooting technique, and the best method to achieve that is through "dry firing" in the comfort of your own home. Dry firing just means firing the gun with an empty chamber or with snap caps (dummy rounds). What is the benefit of this you may wonder? It allows us to refine all aspects of our shooting, from getting into position to aiming, trigger release, and follow through without the distractions of loud "bangs" and recoil. By dry firing, we can more closely examine our technique and catch mistakes that we might not have noticed with the added noise and recoil of live fire.

For example, say you want to check if you are holding your handgun properly and are a bit concerned that you are over-gripping (which would result in shots low and to the side, as we mentioned in Chapter 3). With your unloaded gun, stand facing a blank wall and do everything as if you were firing a loaded gun, and carefully self-examine each step of the process. When you get into position, are your knees locked or are you in a crouched, tense position (remember, we don't want either)? As you lift the handgun, is your supporting arm doing the lifting? Is your front sight focused and crystal clear in the sight picture? When it comes to your grip, do you feel any pressure in your fingertips and are your fingertips turning white? And finally, when the trigger breaks (after what should have been a press straight to the rear), did the front sight you were focused on jerk to the side or did it stay completely still and undisturbed (a blank white wall serves as an excellent target for practicing your trigger release and makes it easy to determine if the front sight moved)? Answer the questions you ask yourself at each step, and the rest is all about practice and adjustments to get to a perfect shot. And of course, with practice (and rhythm and repetition) you will also build fluidity and speed, all while maintaining correct form and technique. Trust me, the results will show on the range and in the field.

It also helps to stick a small target on your wall, one that appears no larger than your front sight in your sight picture. This is a great tool to practice your aiming (focused and clear front sight with a blurry rear sight and target) and your hold. It is also great for natural point of aim exercises.

I think you would be hard pressed to find any top-level marksman that doesn't dry fire more than s/he live fires. The benefits are immense. It is also a great way to stay in shooting "shape" if you don't have time to go to the shooting range as often as you would like. And the price of ammo - especially for certain calibers - can make it unreasonable to train "live" very often. For an alternative solution to these last two constraints (and many more benefits) be sure to read Chapter 10 about airguns.

And one final note: please read your owner's manual and make sure your gun is safe to dry fire. Most modern centerfire guns are, but rimfire guns (like a .22LR) will be damaged by dry firing, unless snap caps are used.

◆ ◆ ◆

Can You Find My Dry Firing Target?

On the following page is the target I use for dry firing with my handguns. The black center appears about the same size as the front sight when standing at the other end of the living room. Just be prepared to answer questions from unsuspecting guests as to why there is a target on your living room wall. I've even had people ask if it was part of the wall design!

◆ ◆ ◆

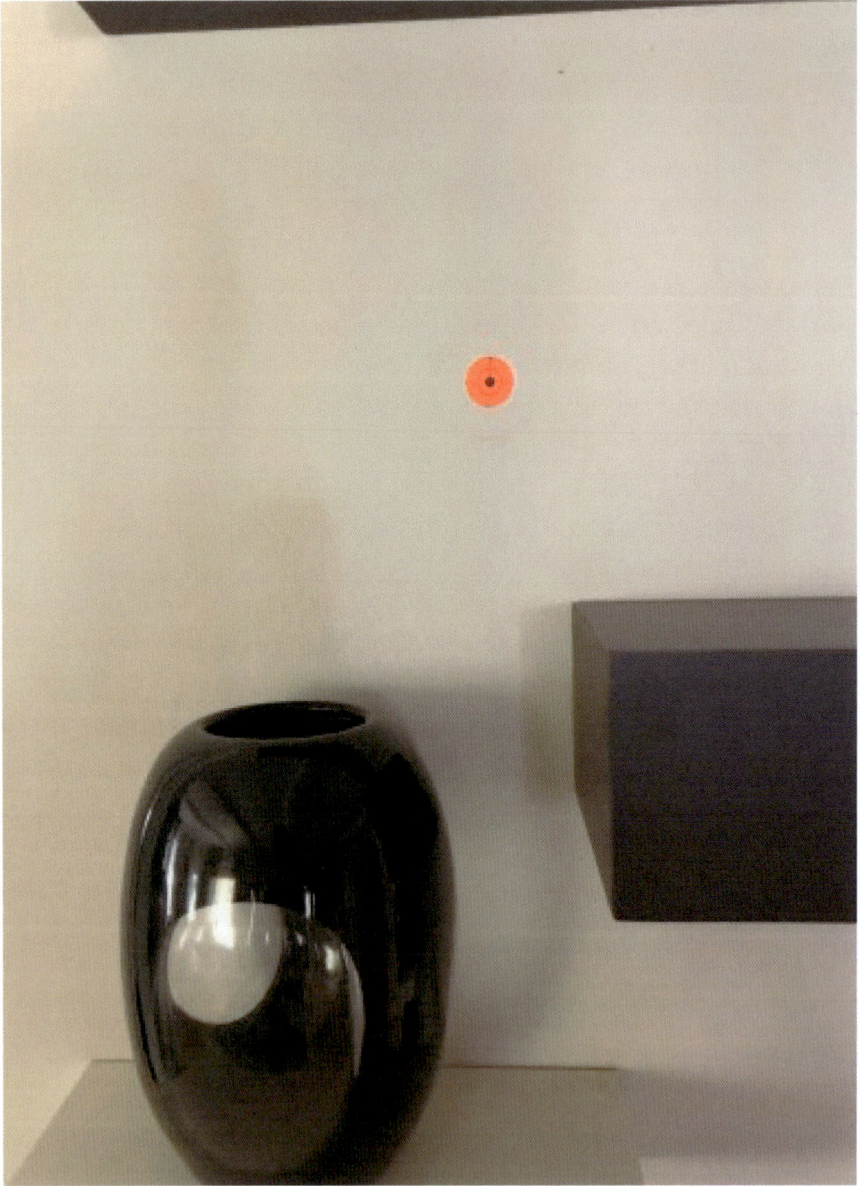

CHAPTER 10 - THE CASE FOR AIRGUNS

Unfortunately, airguns tend to be dismissed as mere "toys" by many firearm owners. I think Ralphie's Red Ryder in *A Christmas Story* played no small part in convincing Americans every Christmas Eve that shooting an airgun would ultimately result in a ricochet and, like Ralphie, in us shooting our eye/glasses out. But all kidding aside, the notion of all airguns being toys couldn't be further from the truth. Many modern airguns are extremely accurate - and often powerful - tools that can be used for hunting, target shooting, and for general practice to become a better marksman with a firearm. I am an enthusiastic proponent of shooting airguns both as a means for building proficiency with firearms as well as for enjoying a challenging and fun sport.

The Daystate Huntsman Revere air rifle in the picture above is extremely accurate and quiet, yet powerful enough for small game hunting.

Many airguns are "backyard friendly," and this translates directly to more live fire practice in the comfort of your own house (please check your local laws first and the patience of your neighbors if they are close by, and set a safe backstop.) In fact, airguns are a great middle step between dry fire practice and shooting your firearm at the shooting range. Besides providing more trigger time, airguns are much quieter and have significantly less recoil than most firearms, thus also providing a great live fire opportunity to cement the techniques we practiced when dry firing with much more subdued disruptions (noise and recoil) compared to shooting firearms.

Another benefit is that nowadays there are quite a few quality airguns that are made to look, feel, and function as close to the firearm models they are replicating as possible and cost only a fraction of the firearm's price. The Umarex built air pistols modeled after the Beretta 92FS and the Smith & Wesson 586 revolver are worth mentioning. Whether we are shooting the "twin" airgun in our backyard, shooting the firearm at the gun range, or dry firing with either in our living room, we are practicing with two guns that feel almost identical in the hand. This is a big advantage because the grip and trigger press that we practice and perfect on the airgun in the backyard carry over almost identically to the firearm. And with the price difference between pellets and powder-burning ammo, I think you will prefer shooting your airgun. To illustrate, a tin of 500 match-grade, German-made pellets cost less than $20. In contrast, 9mm Luger ammo costs around 20-30 cents a round, and ammo for my .243 Winchester hunting rifle goes for over a dollar a round. Airguns provide cheap, and yet greatly beneficial and applicable practice for shooting your firearm.

I started the previous chapter with a surprising statement, and I'll end this chapter with one too. If you master shooting airguns, you will also have mastered shooting most any firearm! To better understand why this is, let us revisit our discussion from Chapter 6 about the bullet or pellet remaining in the barrel for a split second after the trigger is released. I briefly mentioned that the time the projectile spends in the barrel varies depending on the caliber, the ammunition, and the firearm. When we consider airguns as well, we will note that, when compared to firearms, airguns generally have much lower muzzle velocities (meaning the pellet exits the barrel at a slower speed). And this also means that for a firearm and an airgun that have barrels of similar lengths, the slower pellet exiting the airgun necessarily spends a longer amount of time in the barrel.

What does all this matter to the shooter? I think you already know. The longer the projectile spends in the barrel, the more our every mistake is amplified and the more important proper techniques and follow through become. In essence, the airgun, despite many readers' preconceptions, is much less forgiving than a firearm, especially one in a fast caliber. Learn to please this demanding enchantress, and you will have mastered the fundamentals of good shooting.

10 meter Olympic air pistol, along with the 50 meter free pistol, is widely considered to be one of the most difficult disciplines in the shooting sports and one that offers a display of pure marksmanship and precision shooting. The satisfaction of a well-executed shot makes the effort worth it.

◆ ◆ ◆

Remarkable Precision

Airguns can be unbelievably precise. Below is the 5 shot factory test target (5 separate shots went through that one hole) shot from 10 meters that came with my Steyr match air pistol (the same model used by many Olympic athletes). On a bad day, this serves as a stern reminder that the fault rests not with the gun, but with the shooter, me.

◆ ◆ ◆

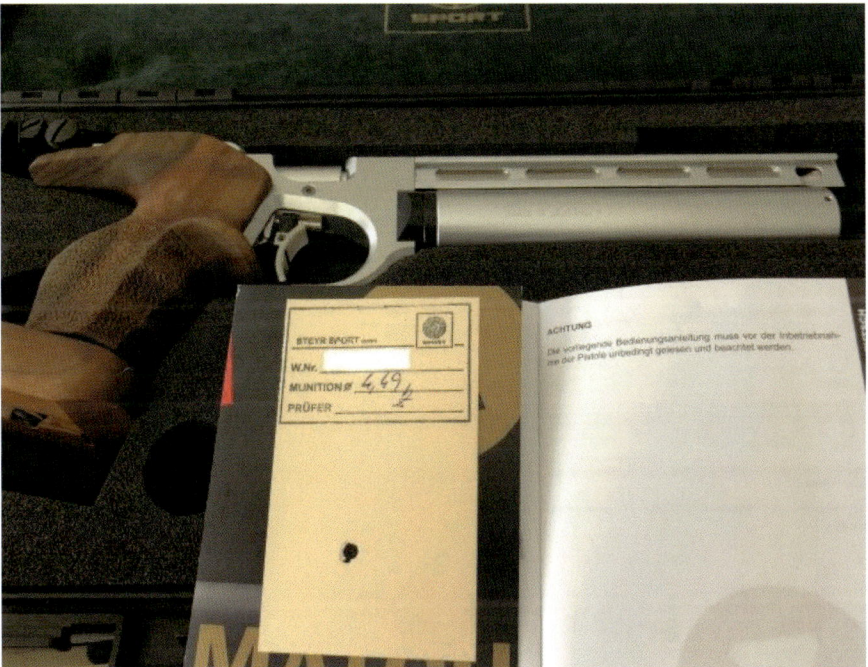

CHAPTER 11 - TIPS AND SUGGESTIONS ON GUNS AND SETTING UP

I would like to wrap up this handbook with a discussion of things to consider when purchasing a rifle or handgun and setting it up for hunting or recreational target shooting.

RIFLES

Let's start with some things to consider when selecting a rifle, and I'll focus our discussion on hunting/back country defense rifles.

Fit

First and foremost, a rifle needs to fit us well if we are to shoot it well, and this is where the term "extension of your body" comes to mind. That's a how a well-fitting rifle should feel like. If we want to get peak performance out of a car for example, we will first make sure our seat is well-adjusted and we can comfortably reach the steering wheel and pedals before we start considering horse-power and other variables. It is no different with a rifle. The rifle should be comfortable to shoot from various positions, and the shooter should be able to comfortably reach the trigger and cycle the bolt without taking the stock off the shoulder or the cheek off the stock. The most important measurement to consider here is the rifle's length of pull (LOP), and this is the distance from the rifle's butt pad to the trigger. While there are some rules of thumb for approximating the optimal length of pull for our body, there is no substitute for testing a rifle in-person. Generally, the LOP of modern production rifles tends to lean a bit on the long side for a person of average build (logic being that a gunsmith can shorten the stock, if needed), and most military issue rifles tend to be on the shorter side (logic being that recruits of all shapes and sizes should be able to reach the trigger, even if that causes some inconveniences). Luckily, nowadays there are a plethora of aftermarket parts for fit adjustment including adjustable stocks, spacers, and cheek risers for many of the big-brand produced rifles.

Weight

While we need to of course consider the intended use of the rifle, the bottom line here is that we are not going to get very far lugging around a heavy rifle. That bull-barreled rifle that might be great for shooting strings of small groups is not going to do us any favors when we're carrying it through the woods. A lighter rifle is also faster to handle. The average wood-stocked hunting rifle weighs around seven to eight pounds, and although that might not seem heavy at first, we need to also consider the weight of the scope, rings, and sling that will be mounted on. This can easily push the weight of the overall rig to the nine to ten pound range. There are now more and more rifles manufactured with synthetic stocks and lighter contoured barrels in the six pound or less range, and trust me when I say that those one to two pounds make a world of difference in carrying comfort and handling speed. As a personal example, the first higher-end hunting rifle I bought was my Winchester Model 70 Supergrade, and while it is a gorgeous gun with a beautiful, blued finish and a high-grade walnut stock, it is rather heavy. If I am going hunting and I know I'll likely be covering a lot of ground, I'll reach for my significantly lighter Weatherby rifle instead.

One thing to keep in mind though with lighter rifles is that they tend to be less forgiving to shoot well because any body movement and uneven tension will tend to disrupt a lighter rifle more easily than a heavier rifle that has "settled" into a steady hold. And a lighter rifle will feel as though it is kicking harder because there is less weight to absorb the recoil, though stock design plays a key factor in felt recoil as well. As always, practice is key!

Caliber

Ultra-fast or ultra-powerful calibers tend to get a lot of hype and tend to attract a significant number of less-experienced shooters who believe they are getting an advantage with a gun chambered in that caliber. What they fail to consider is the price of recoil. If a gun recoils so hard that it causes the shooter to flinch, the shooter will likely miss the target, and the speed or the power of the bullet will not matter at all. **Buy a gun in a caliber that you are comfortable shooting.** I cannot stress this enough. It's common to find rifles in like-new condition chambered in African dangerous game calibers like the .375 H&H or the .416 Rigby on the used gun rack presumably because the buyer decided to sell the gun after taking only a couple shots and experiencing the painful recoil.

Nowadays there are plenty of versatile cartridges that are capable of taking down most North American big game (except large bears) and are perfectly suitable for most target shooting applications that also produce recoil that can be quite comfortably handled by most people. The 6.5mm Creedmoor, 7mm-08 Remington, and .308 Winchester are just a few examples that come to mind. To drive the point home that "bigger" isn't always necessary, I'll mention that the legendary, turn of the century African hunter W.D.M "Karamojo" Bell regularly used a rifle chambered in 7x57mm Mauser (a popular military round in the late 19th and early 20th centuries and similar to today's 7mm-08 Remington) to hunt elephants (of course, he knew where to place his shots). By no means am I suggesting you walk around the grizzly woods on your own armed with only a 7mm-08 Remington rifle. But what I am saying is that shooters should consider that perhaps a rifle chambered for a less powerful cartridge will suffice for the intended task, especially taking into account the advancements in modern gunpowder and bullet technology.

Trigger Weight

Trigger weight is the weight of the resistance measured in pounds and ounces required to overcome until the trigger breaks, thus releasing the sear and firing the shot. We discussed in Chapter 3 that the objective of a clean trigger press is to press the trigger and release the shot without disturbing our aim and sight picture, and this is more easily achieved with a light trigger that has a crisp, consistent breaking point. This applies to rifles, handguns, and really to any precision instrument with a release mechanism. A lighter trigger requires less muscle tension to press, and thus reduces the likelihood of the trigger press adversely affecting our shot. It allows for faster, more precise shooting.

Luckily, quite a number of new, affordable hunting rifles have very respectable, crisp sporting triggers in the three-pound weight range that are a pleasure to shoot. Savage's AccuTrigger is especially noteworthy. Most service handguns on the other hand come out of the factory with heavier and grittier triggers that require more practice to shoot well. And comparing the triggers on modern hunting rifles to the triggers on military issue rifles and handguns from the turn of the 20th century shows just how much superior modern units are. After being spoiled with the triggers on top-notch match airguns, I sometimes wonder how I tolerated the trigger of my Mosin-Nagant when that was the only firearm I owned.

There are also reputable manufacturers (Timney Triggers are great) that specialize in building high quality trigger mechanisms for many popular rifles and handguns and offering them as aftermarket replacement options that an experienced gunowner or gunsmith can install. If I'm tinkering with a gun, the trigger is usually the first thing I'll replace or have tuned by a competent gunsmith (but only if I feel it is necessary after dry firing the gun several hundred times). And often it is the only thing I'll feel the need to tinker with.

Ultimately, any trigger can be mastered with sufficient dry fire practice, but selecting a gun with a good trigger from the get-go is even better.

A couple points of caution that should be mentioned, however: A very light trigger can be dangerous and potentially lead to an accidental discharge. Very light triggers under a pound are suitable for target shooting only. And second, unless you absolutely know what you are doing, please take your gun to an experienced gunsmith if you would like any work done to it. Trigger work especially should be handled with the utmost care because the consequences of an accidental discharge can be disastrous.

Scopes and Rings

Without going into a detailed discussion on the topic, I will say that most scopes from reputable manufacturers (Leupold, Vortex, Bushnell, etc.) are well made products. Unless you have a specific need, don't fall for the hype of high magnification scopes with target turrets and heavily marked reticles geared for the long-range shooting crowd. A few hundred yards shot is not considered long range with modern day rifles and scopes, and we have no need other than for a simple, robust optic.

For most hunting and recreational target shooting applications, a variable power scope in the popular 3-9 times magnification range with a 40 mm objective and duplex reticle is perfectly sufficient. I like having a lower magnification no higher than 3 times because of the wider field of view (and thus faster target acquisition) the scope provides. When I was taking a rifle class at Gunsite Academy, I had the opportunity to shoot a Steyr Scout rifle mated to a Leupold 2.5 power fixed magnification scope. The scope's small size and weight kept the rifle light, and the lower magnification provided a wide field of view and allowed me to find the target right away. And the 2.5 times magnification was more than enough for shots on plate size targets out to 300 yards.

However, scopes have their own quirks and intricacies - parallax, first focal plane vs second focal plane are a couple that come to mind – that are beyond the scope of this book (pun intended) but that the serious-minded marksman should research and understand before purchasing a scope for his/her rifle.

Regarding rings to attach the scope to the rifle, please buy a quality pair of rings. These rings are what hold the scope fixed to your rifle and are no place to "cheap out" on. I like Talley rings and integrated mounts, though many of the large scope manufacturers also manufacture rings for use with their scopes.

A final consideration to highlight here is the height of the rings;

generally, we want rings that position the scope as low to the rifle as possible without the scope's objective touching the barrel or the scope interfering with the operation of the bolt. This low position of the scope to the rifle will aid with maintaining a proper cheek weld on the stock and alignment of the scope with our eye.

Mounting and Leveling a Scope

There are many YouTube videos and step by step articles on how to mount and level a scope, so I will keep this summary brief.

Before we get started with the final mounting and leveling procedure, we want to make sure the scope will be positioned on the rifle with correct eye relief (the distance between the rear lens of the scope and our eye) when shooting from various positions. To do this, let's attach the rings to the rifle and set the scope in the rings. Do not tighten the screws for this exercise; we want to be able to move the scope back and forth within the rings. Next, let's assume various shooting positions (sitting, standing, prone, etc.) and move the scope back and forth until we find the optimal position of the scope where our sight picture is clear and there is no scope "shadow" (black areas in our view when looking through the scope). And be sure to try this exercise at high and low magnifications if you have a variable power scope, since eye relief is reduced at higher magnifications. We want ample eye relief both to avoid the scope hitting our brow in recoil and to have a clear sight picture from multiple positions.

One more tip: do not set scope position from the bench (unless benchrest is the only type of shooting you plan to do). Adjusting the scope placement for convenient eye relief from that shooting position will likely place the scope too far back for proper eye relief from other shooting positions, and you might end up with a cut or bruised eyebrow to show for it. Finally, mark the scope with a pencil where it should be positioned in the rings for optimal eye relief.

Now let's go about the process of leveling. We'll start by first leveling the rifle to the Earth and then the scope to the Earth (and ultimately both should also be level to each other if nothing moves).

We need to first secure the rifle in a vise. If you are using a generic bench vise and not a dedicated gun vise, I recommend placing a couple pieces of wood and soft cloth as padding between the vice's jaws and the rifle to avoid scratching the stock. Then place a small level (bubble or digital) on a flat surface on the receiver of the rifle. This will usually be the scope base or if you are using an integrated base and ring mount like the Talley unit I have on both of my rifles pictured in Chapter 2, then attach and tighten the bottom half of the rings to the rifle and place the level on either the front or rear bottom half ring (or try both for good measure). The bottom half of the rings will serve as the "next best" flat surface to use as a proxy to level the rifle. Next, let's slightly loosen the vise and adjust the cant of the rifle until the rifle is perfectly level. With a bubble level, the bubble should be directly in the center of the level, or if a digital level is used, it should show an angle of zero degrees. And now we need to tighten the vise being careful not to disturb the rifle's level.

At this point the rifle should be level and we need to then level the scope. To do this, we place the scope in the bottom half of the rings and screw in the top half of the rings without tightening the screws. Let's not forget to also align the mark we made on the scope with the rings so that the scope is positioned for optimal eye relief. We then place the level on the elevation turret cap (or preferably directly on the turret, if the top of the turret is flat) and turn the scope left or right until it is perfectly level. You can double check the scope's level by hanging a piece of string with a weight attached to it some distance in front of the rifle. The vertical crosshair should be parallel to the string. (At the risk of going into too much detail, I'll caveat this by saying that occasionally, a scope's crosshairs might be canted and not perfectly aligned with the elevation and windage turrets – there are manufacturing tolerances for this. My suggestion is that if the scope is perfectly level according to the level on the turret but the vertical crosshair is visibly not parallel to the hanging string, you should exchange that scope for another one.)

Again, be careful not to move the rifle throughout this process or else you'll need to redo the entire exercise.

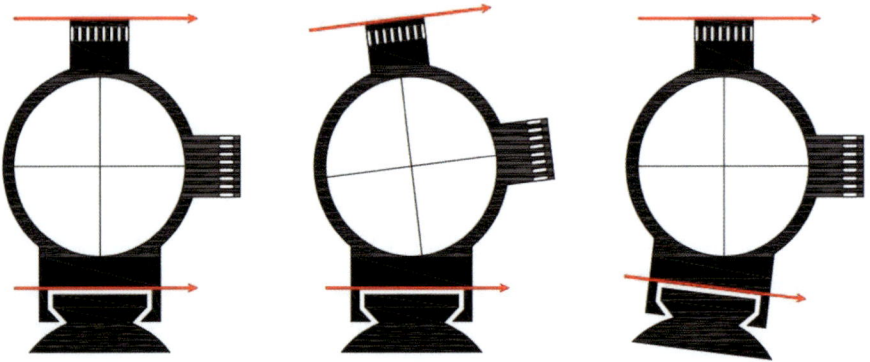

The rifle and scope are perfectly level in the image on the left. That is the result we want. As long as we are holding the rifle level when shooting, we can use either the turrets or reticle holdover to precisely adjust for windage and elevation; each turret click will move point of impact exactly vertically or horizontally and using the reticle for holdover will do the same. With a canted rifle or canted scope (which would introduce rifle cant when we rotate the rifle to level the scope), our shots will drift to the side and low, especially as distance increases (explained in Chapter 8). And adjustments with the turrets or reticle holdover will move point of impact at an angle, not vertically or horizontally.

Finally, let's tighten the ring screws, again being careful not to move either the rifle or the scope out of alignment. Follow an X pattern when tightening the screws to apply even pressure from all sides.

If you have a torque wrench, use it to tighten the screws to the manufacturer's specifications. If you don't own one, no need to worry. Just remember that we want a secure connection of the scope to the rifle without applying too much torque that might damage the scope. If using the typical small wrenches supplied with the scope, firm, "finger-tight" pressure should suffice. Remember, we aren't torquing a wheel to a car's axle here. I've mounted multiple scopes prior to purchasing a torque wrench and haven't had a scope move from recoil or be damaged from over-torquing. (Some shooters prefer to apply Blue Loctite to the threads of the screws to prevent the screws from loosening. I usually apply it on the base screws that attach the rings to the rifle but not on the ring screws that tighten the scope in place. Properly torqued screws will not easily loosen.) Don't overthink it. And now we are ready to sight in our rifle.

Here I demonstrate the final result of the leveling exercise with a break-barrel air rifle, but the concept applies to powder-burning rifles as well. The bubble level on the squared off surface of the breech confirms the level of the rifle, and the bubble level on the turret confirms the level of the scope. If the breech did not have a flat, horizontal surface and there wasn't a scope rail on the receiver, I would use the bottom half of the rings as the

next best alternative to level the rifle and be careful not to move
the rifle when leveling the scope and tightening the rings.

Sighting in the Rifle

We want to sight in our rifle from as steady a position as possible, and I recommend using a sandbag rest for optimal results – just remember to rest the fore-end of the stock and never the barrel on the bag (we don't want to disturb barrel harmonics and thus consistency). And we want to make sure to hold the rifle as level as possible throughout the exercise (and of course thereafter).

Because the scope is not yet "zeroed in", the point of aim and point of impact might diverge significantly. I recommend placing the target close by at around 25 yards for the first sighter shots to ensure that we "hit paper" (bullet impacts somewhere on the target). Shoot at least two shots (preferably a group of three) to reliably note the center of the group prior to making any adjustments. Now we can calibrate the scope. Let's measure the horizontal and vertical distance from the center of the shot group to the center of the bullseye. This is similar in concept to how we would count up/down and left/right on a XY coordinate grid. In fact, some targets have a coordinate grid with one-inch squares printed on them to aid in measuring vertical and horizontal distance to the bullseye.

Most scopes for the American market utilize minutes of angle (MOA) adjustments. Without going into more trigonometry, I'll just say that a one MOA adjustment practically equates to a one-inch shift in point of impact at 100 yards. The magnitude of the shifts increases proportionally with distance, so at 200 yards a one MOA adjustment would move the point of impact by two inches. Most MOA scopes allow for adjustments at $1/4$ MOA, meaning that a one-click turn of either the elevation or windage turret moves the point of impact by $1/4$ of an inch at 100 yards in the corresponding direction.

Returning to our target at 25 yards, one click of the turret would proportionally translate to a $1/16^{th}$ -inch adjustment (25 yards is $1/4$ the distance of 100 yards, and so $1/4$ of a $1/4$ of an inch adjustment is 1/16th of an inch). So, if at 25 yards our point of impact landed 2 inches to the left and 3 inches low of the center of the bullseye (see the following image of the target), we would dial the windage turret 32 clicks to the right and the elevation turret 48 clicks up. In theory, our next shot should hit dead center of the bullseye. However, don't be surprised if the next few shots still land just a bit away from the bullseye. Most scopes don't offer precisely ¼ MOA adjustments as marketed; my experience with most scopes has been that each click moves the point of impact slightly more than ¼ MOA. But any quality scope will offer consistent adjustments, and as we already know from reading this book, consistency is what matters.

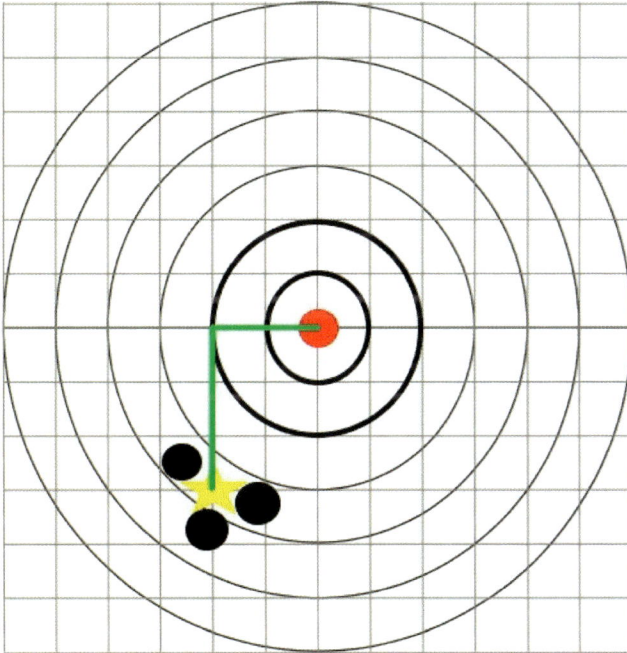

And remember, we don't necessarily want to zero in our scope to hit the center of the bullseye at 25 yards. Decide at what distance you want the far zero to be (the second time the bullet crosses the line of sight), and then use a trajectory table as discussed in Chapter 8 to determine how much below the line of sight the bullet should impact at 25 yards. Then of course move the target back to that far zero distance to fine tune any adjustments and confirm that point of aim and impact indeed align.

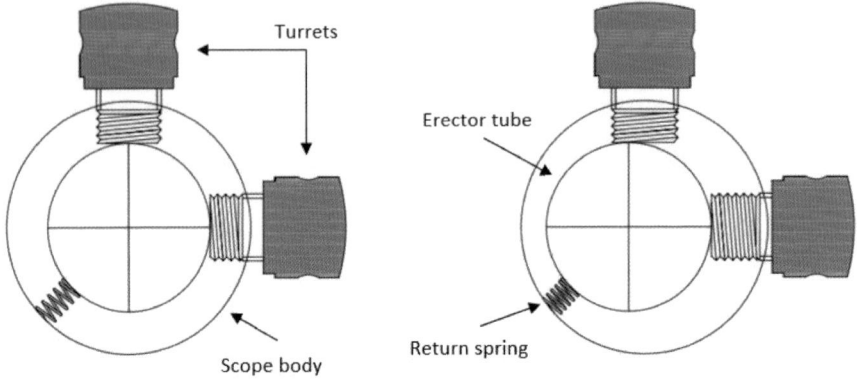

Turrets are essentially fine screws that are used to move the erector tube within the scope (and in turn the reticle) so that our point of aim aligns with the point of impact. When our rifle is sighted in (in the absence of external variables like wind), the vertical crosshair should exactly bisect the rifle's bore.

Furthermore, we should sight in the gun with the same ammunition we intend to use for our desired application, be that hunting or target shooting. Even for the same caliber, different manufacturers (and even one manufacturer in particular) may produce ammunition with different bullet weights, shapes, construction, and muzzle velocity, and differences in these variables may result in different trajectories and points of impact. The difference in point of impact will be negligible at 25 yards, likely slight at 100, but can become significant as distance increases. I also recommend trying a few different loads to determine which ammunition shoots the most precisely out of your rifle. Certain characteristics of the rifle, especially the rate of twist of the barrel's rifling, can influence how the rifle stabilizes the bullet. It may stabilize one bullet type better than another, and this impacts precision as well (see more on twist rates below). It may also help to read ammunition reviews online or search some firearm and shooting forums because avid shooters will often share how certain factory ammunition performed out of their rifle and include specifics such as the make and model of their rifle or the twist rate of the barrel. And having that extra confidence that the rifle and ammunition combination will precisely do their part if we do ours is always a good thing.

Finally, if you plan to shoot using a sling but sighted in your rifle rested on a sandbag, please spend some time shooting with the sling from various positions and noting the point of impact. The tension from the sling will likely change the rifle's recoil pattern a bit and cause shots to land slightly lower than when shot resting the rifle on a sandbag.

Twist Rate

This topic belongs in a more advanced discussion, but I mention it here because in some cases it may be the root cause of a rifle shooting certain ammunition strikingly inaccurately and leaving the less experienced marksman frustrated and perplexed as to why that is happening. Especially now that a growing number of states either require or strongly recommend the use of lead-free ammunition for hunting, we'll see that twist rate may be something we'll want to take a closer look at when purchasing a rifle.

We know that all rifles have spiral grooves running through the barrel called rifling - hence the term *rifle*. Their purpose is to stabilize the bullet to travel through the air more accurately and consistently; the rifling serves the same purposes as putting a spin on a football throw.

But not all rifling is created equal. Rifles in different calibers and even for the same caliber can have barrels with rifling in different twist rates, in other words the rate of spin of the rifling measured in inches per turn. For example, a twist rate of 1:10 means that the rifling (and hence the bullet) completes one full revolution in the barrel every ten inches. And a 1:9 twist would signify that one revolution is completed every nine inches, resulting in a faster rate of spin.

There is a relationship between the projectile's (bullet's) length and velocity and the twist rate required for optimal stability. Let's focus on the length variable. Longer bullets need faster twist rates to stabilize the bullet. What does that mean for us? Bullet shape and material being constant, we can deduce that of two bullets of the same caliber but of varying weights, the heavier bullet would necessarily be longer, since the diameter of the bullet is also constant due to the fixed diameter of the barrel; weight can be added only by making a longer bullet. And given that a longer bullet needs a faster twist rate for optimal stability, we can now recognize that it may not shoot as accurately out of a barrel with a twist rate optimized for bullets of lighter or intermediate weight for caliber.

Let's now consider lead-free ammunition and its ramifications on required twist rate. Lead-free bullets are made of either copper or zinc or some combination of the two, and either material is less dense than lead; a one cubic inch block of cooper or zinc will weigh less than one cubic inch of lead. So, if we want a copper bullet that is close to the same weight as a traditional lead-core bullet of the same caliber, the copper bullet must necessarily be longer just as in the earlier example. We can already surmise that likely a barrel in a faster twist rate will be necessary to shoot that bullet accurately. Luckily, many ammunition manufacturers will list the recommended barrel twist rate for a certain factory load. But as a rule, if we plan to predominantly shoot or hunt with heavy or lead-free rounds, it is a good idea to purchase a rifle with a fast-for-caliber twist rate.

◆ ◆ ◆

A Tale Of Two Twist Rates

Believe it or not, twist rate played an integral part in the rise of one of today's most popular hunting rounds, and the demise of another. In 1955 Winchester and Remington introduced very similar calibers: the .243 Winchester and the .244 Remington, respectively. Both fired 6mm bullets, but Winchester offered the caliber in its Model 70 rifle with a 1:10 twist rate while Remington chose a 1:12 twist rate in its rifle. While both calibers were advertised as being suitable for varmints and deer-sized game, Winchester's factory loads came in bullet weights up to 100 grains, while Remington limited the weight of the bullets in its factory loads to no heavier than 90 grains, because the slower twist rate would not reliably stabilize bullets that were any heavier. Hunters preferred bullets of at least 100 grains for use on deer and noticed that Remington did not offer such bullets in factory loads, and handloaders concluded that bullets of that weight would not stabilize in Remington rifles anyway. Then word spread. Today the .243 Winchester is as popular as ever, but few people remember the .244 Remington. And to end with a somewhat expected twist to the story (pun intended), some of the heavier lead-free .243 Winchester loads that are seeing wider use today due to hunting regulations do not reliably stabilize in barrels with a 1:10 twist rate, and several manufacturers now offer rifles chambered in .243 Winchester with a 1:9 twist rate as a result.

◆ ◆ ◆

HANDGUNS

Most of the topics discussed about rifles apply for handguns as well.

The handgun's fit to our hand is especially important because poor fit can result in us not being able to press the trigger straight to the rear. Take the Beretta 92 FS, for example. While it is inherently a very accurate handgun, it has a grip that is too thick and a trigger too far forward for some. On the other hand, the CZ 75 is lauded for a grip that universally fits most people well. There is a large aftermarket for grip insets, trigger blades, and many other parts to customize many popular handguns to our fit and liking.

I will repeat what I said about choice of caliber for added emphasis: go with a caliber you are comfortable shooting. There is a plethora of great handguns chambered in the popular 9mm Luger round which can be ideal for both home defense and recreational shooting, and most people should be able to shoot this caliber comfortably. For revolvers the .357 Magnum is a great choice because we can fire both the potent .357 Magnum round but also the much softer-shooting .38 Special round out of the same handgun. And while Clint Eastwood in Dirty Harry made shooting a .44 Magnum look cool and sent customers scrambling to buy one, the reality is that most people cannot handle that powerful round comfortably.

Regarding size and weight, my suggestion here would be to avoid the ultra-light or pocket-sized handguns, unless you have a specific need for such a handgun. The drawback of handguns that are too light, like rifles but to a greater extent, is that they are harder to hold steady, especially when pressing the typically heavy and gritty triggers on these guns. And felt recoil is greater and can easily become uncomfortable. Smaller handguns also have shorter sight radiuses (the distance between the front and rear sights), and thus are more difficult to aim precisely.

In terms of sighting in a handgun, many service pistols come with fixed sights that, in my experience, are well fitted to ensure point of aim and impact alignment with a center hold at distances between 25 and 50 yards. If your handgun comes with screw adjustable sights, then all the better. The exercise to calibrate the sights is similar to how we sighted in a rifle scope, except that we turn small screws, not turrets, and that the adjustments are generally coarser.

CLOSING REMARKS

Congratulations on making it to the end of my handbook - I am glad I didn't lose you at the trajectory chapter. I hope you found this guide useful and informative. Please practice the material in this book safely and responsibly. With that in mind, I hope you become a proficient and skilled marksman and continue in the pursuit of precision.

Please reach out at "precisionshootingschool" and "precisionshootingschool@gmail.com," via Instagram and email, respectively.

Best wishes and shoot straight!

ACKNOWLEDGEMENTS AND RECOMMENDATIONS FOR FURTHER READING

I have listed below other writings on rifle and handgun shooting that I referenced or quoted in this book. They are also, in my opinion, excellent resources for the inquisitive marksman that wants to learn more about the shooting sports.

Ways of the Rifle **by Gaby Buhlmann, Heinz Reinkemeier et al. MEC, 2008**

Though a book specifically on Olympic three position small bore and air rifle shooting, this book provides a wealth of information that can be applied to rifle shooting in general. It reviews the prone, standing, and kneeling positions in great detail and takes a magnifying glass view to many of the other topics we discussed here. I would consider it a must read for the serious rifle shooter.

The Art of the Rifle **by Jeff Cooper. Paladin Press, 1997**

The Art of the Rifle does a good job reviewing shooting positions for shooting in the field and other practical considerations. It also contains a good overview on the use of the shooting sling and its varieties. But Jeff Cooper does not discuss topics in the depth that

Buhlmann and Reinkemeier do in *Ways of the Rifle.* Overall, the book is a favorite among many, likely due in no small part to Jeff Cooper's legacy as the founder of Gunsite Academy and his role in the development of the two-handed "modern technique" for defensive pistol shooting.

Long Range Shooting Handbook: The Complete Beginner's Guide to Precision Rifle Shooting by Ryan Cleckner. North Shadow Press, 2016

I had come across Cleckner's book multiple times before, but I ordered it only just before publishing this second edition to read through and review for my readers. And I can say that I wholeheartedly recommend it. Cleckner reviews shooting positions and sling use and discusses shooting fundamentals with an emphasis on consistency and being relaxed much like this book does, but he focuses the discussion on long range shooting as the title suggests and dives into some topics that are relevant only for that application. Cleckner does a great job breaking down concepts in easy-to-understand terms and examples. His book is a great add to your shooting library, especially if you have an interest in long range shooting.

Pistol Shooting The Olympic Disciplines by Heinz Reinkemeier and Gaby Buhlmann. MEC, 2013

Another work by Reinkemeier and Buhlmann, and it is a masterclass on pistol shooting. Again, geared for the Olympic shooting crowd, it goes into every minute detail of shooting position, aiming, trigger press, follow through and much more, leaving no stone unturned. And the book contains more than 1200 photos to reinforce the discussions. I highly recommend this book.

The Perfect Pistol Shot by Albert H. League III. Paladin Press, 2011

This is a great book on practical pistol shooting for the beginner. It is a quick and easy read, and League does a great job with "Prove it" exercises and Q&A sections that are included in every chapter to drive home shooting fundamentals. This was the first book I bought on handgun shooting, and it helped me develop my shooting.

Practical Shooting: Beyond Fundamentals by Brian Enos. Zediker Publishing, 1990

Brian Enos dives deep into practical pistol shooting and in addition to being a comprehensive reference on the subject, his book is a treatise on how to think about shooting. Enos shares with us his philosophy on shooting and discusses important observations in the shooting process like our awareness, focus, and details that we may not initially consider but that can help us self-diagnose our own shooting if we are aware of them. This book is well worth the read.

Airgun Academy Blog by Tom Gaylord, Writing as B.B. Pelletier

Tom Gaylord is a legend in the airgun community for his role in introducing airguns as serious tools for target shooting and hunting to the general shooting public. His blogs are a pleasure to read, and they are peppered with great advice on shooting techniques. When I started my shooting hobby with an air rifle, Tom Gaylord's blog had a big influence on my technique development; I would read his blog and then test what I read right in the backyard!

Gunsite Academy. Paulden, Arizona

This isn't a book you can read of course, but Gunsite Academy is the most renowned and oldest shooting school in the nation that offers training to both civilians and military/law enforcement personnel. The academy's catalogue of weeklong training courses run the gamut from focusing on rifles, handguns, long range shooting and more, and they offer something for shooters of all skill levels. Regardless of your background, I think you will walk out a better marksman than when you walked in. For me the most valuable part of the rifle course I took were running the simulation drills which replicated real-life hunting scenarios under time pressure. Gunsite also provides a great opportunity to have a fun time with people that share similar interests, and many lasting friendships are made there.

Printed in Great Britain
by Amazon

79955086R00056